MEASURING THE IMPACT OF MANPOWER PROGRAMS
A Primer

POLICY PAPERS IN HUMAN RESOURCES
AND INDUSTRIAL RELATIONS 17

W9-CZU-831

Michael E. Borus
MICHIGAN STATE UNIVERSITY

William R. Tash
U. S. DEPARTMENT OF LABOR

ANN ARBOR, MICHIGAN
NOVEMBER 1970

INSTITUTE OF LABOR AND INDUSTRIAL RELATIONS
THE UNIVERSITY OF MICHIGAN—WAYNE STATE UNIVERSITY

CONTENTS

331.112
B648m
Cop. 3

PREFACE

This study was originally prepared for the Office of Evaluation, Manpower Administration, U. S. Department of Labor, when Borus was a Brookings Institution Economic Policy Fellow and Tash was Chief of the Methodology Section. Its purpose was primarily to present ideas for the measurement of the impact of manpower programs, to foster discussion and stimulate the development of an improved methodology for assessing results of manpower programs. This monograph, however, represents only one of many possible approaches to measuring certain impacts of manpower programs. As such, it reflects the views of the authors and should not be considered to be the officially established policy of the Manpower Administration.

Many people within the Labor Department made substantive contributions to this primer. Special mention should be made of the contributions of Paul Barton, John Cheston, Audrey Freedman, Frank Lewis, Blossom Reutlinger, Frank Shuler, Ralph Walker, Barbara Weinstein, Alfred Zuck, and especially Abraham Stahler. We would also like to thank Mary Melton who typed many versions of this work. Finally, we would like to extend our appreciation to the persons outside of the Labor Department who were kind enough to review a draft of the primer and give us their reactions as to the usefulness of the document and any significant changes that might improve it: Don Davis, Garth Mangum, Edward Prescott, Gosta Rehn, and Harold Sheppard. Their reactions, we might add, encouraged us to proceed with publication of the primer.

"The need for effective evaluation is a continuous one, but is especially acute when large amounts of public and private resources are involved and when the consequences of misconceived programs may be far-reaching. In effect, the need for sound methods of evaluation transcends any particular substantive problem. We all need tests and standards that will keep us honest men."*

George P. Shultz
Secretary of Labor

*"Priorities in Policy and Research for Industrial Relations," *Proceedings of the Twenty-first Annual Winter Meeting,* Industrial Relations Research Association, 1969, p. 11.

1

INTRODUCTION

The need for effective evaluation is no more acute than in the field of manpower programs. Nearly four billion dollars were obligated between fiscal years 1963 and 1969, a substantial sum by any standard. More importantly, the lives of over four million program participants were affected. To the extent that manpower programs were inefficient or ineffective, dollars were wasted and workers did not achieve their full potential.

Past Evaluation Procedures

The past evaluations of manpower programs have taken a variety of forms which differed primarily in terms of the variables being measured. Three basic types of evaluations can be identified.[1]

The first type of evaluation is monitoring program operating

---

[1] For another, excellent classification of types of evaluations, see Louis A. Ferman, "Some Perspectives on Evaluating Social Welfare Programs," *The Annals of the American Academy of Political and Social Science*, Vol. 385 (September 1969), pp. 143-156.

efficiency (project monitoring). Project monitoring begins with a basic model which describes how a particular manpower program should be administered. This model will include such items as the qualifications of the program staff, the administrative hierarchy which should be present, the reporting forms which should be used, and the list of services which should be performed. Project monitoring then will seek to determine if the model is being followed and to what extent procedures and practices may be modified to follow more closely the model of operating efficiency.

The second type of evaluation arises out of the need by program operators for immediate information on the success or failure of a particular program. Immediate information is necessary to judge the value of particular program components and personnel within a project and the relative efficiency of different projects. Emphasis is therefore placed on measuring short-run goals which can be examined while a project is in operation, or shortly thereafter. Thus criteria of program success will include such objectives as the learning of new skills, the placement record of the project immediately following its completion, and the improvement in earnings of the program participants as compared with their earnings before the program. Most of the evaluations of manpower programs carried on in the past by the U. S. Department of Labor and Office of Economic Opportunity have been this type of evaluation—measuring the success of a program and of its components in terms of short-run goals.

The third basic type of evaluation (impact evaluation) examines the long-run goals of manpower programs and views success and failure in these terms. It is with this type of evaluation that we will be primarily concerned in this primer, since we believe that it can best provide the sets of information we consider necessary for decision making. There are obviously very real uses of the other types of evaluations. We were not able to treat all three types intensively, however, and have chosen to emphasize the one with which we are most familiar.

Goals of Impact Evaluation

The purpose of the evaluation process is to provide policymakers with the basic data necessary for them to make decisions wisely. Impact evaluations of manpower programs should provide five essential sets of information. First, they should provide all of the data necessary to determine if a particular manpower program should be continued. Second, they should determine which of alternative programs achieve the greatest gains for a given cost. Third, evaluations should present information on the components of each program and the mixes of components which are most effective for a given expenditure so that maximum operating efficiency can be achieved. Fourth, evaluations should provide the first three types of information for persons with different characteristics, so that a decisionmaker may determine which individuals are best served by each program. Finally, in the course of evaluating existing programs, data should be gathered which will suggest new methods to attack manpower problems. To date, no evaluation of manpower programs has provided all of this information.

Approach

In designing this primer we sought to present an introduction to the measurement of manpower program impact. The discussion was to be for the beginner and although some knowledge of research methods was to be assumed the reader was not to be expected to have prior experience with impact evaluations. Consequently, we decided to concentrate on basic techniques and omit much of the theoretical discussions which have occurred in the field of impact evaluation (although references to these discussions would be provided). At the same time, however, we felt that while the techniques for measuring the impact of manpower programs are not difficult to master, most past studies have not included all the basic components necessary to arrive at reliable conclusions which can be used by policymakers with confidence. Therefore, in this monograph we chose to give special emphasis to the areas where past studies have typically failed. The result we hope is an elementary presentation which will help to correct some of the apparent deficiencies in past studies.

One of the major problems in the evaluation of manpower programs is that these programs encompass a wide variety of services for the nation's workers and potential workers. Generally, they seek to improve the employment situation of the program clients and in this way better their economic, physical, and mental well-being. They also seek to increase the productive ability of the nation's human resources and to reduce poverty and social dependency. These goals, however, are broad and difficult to operationalize. Thus the evaluations of manpower programs often have been narrow in focus, usually limited to the most obvious effects of the programs such as increments in earnings by the participants or the number of participants placed in training-related jobs. Other less apparent but possibly important factors have been frequently ignored. Therefore, our first task, in Chapter 2, is to define more of the basic objectives of manpower programs and attempt to establish criteria to measure these objectives.

The designs for measuring the success of manpower programs in past studies have often been weak. Many of the problems have been in the use of control or comparison groups. To estimate the effects of a manpower program, it is necessary to compare the experience of the program participants with that of some reference group who can be said to represent what would have happened to the participants in the absence of the program. Unfortunately, too often the results of past studies have been dismissed on the grounds of noncomparability between program participants and "controls." This problem of comparability has arisen from two sources: (1) the retrospective nature of the studies which requires them to rely on available data, and (2) the lack of knowledge about other groups of persons who may serve as control group members. In Chapter 3, we present a procedure which we feel will best solve the comparability problems. We also supply descriptive data on other possible control groups in the event our procedure cannot be followed.

Other problems which have arisen in manpower program evaluations revolve around the question, "Whom do manpower programs affect?" It appears that past studies have oftentimes excluded, either because of a lack of data or theoretical basis, many persons whose labor market experience was influenced by manpower programs. In Chapter 3 we point out some of the other groups who also should be examined. We also suggest in this chapter a number of technical aspects which have often been lacking in previous studies—the use of multivariate analysis to separate out the influence of the wide variety of possible determinants of program success, the use of marginal analysis whenever possible, and the methods for projecting and discounting future effects of the programs.

The usefulness of the project monitoring and the short-run goals types of evaluation are often limited because no knowledge exists on the efficacy of the criteria of program success used in these studies. These types of studies, however, offer a timeliness which is unavailable from impact evaluations but is most welcome to program operators. Chapter 4 is an attempt to integrate the three types of evaluations to improve the value of all of them.

The problems involved in measuring the costs of manpower programs have been similar to those involved in measuring program success. Past studies have not measured all of the proper costs, the selection of control groups often has been inadequate, not all groups incurring costs have been examined, and multivariate techniques have seldom been used. These are the issues discussed in Chapters 5 and 6.

A final problem which has limited the usefulness of many previous evaluations has been the lack of comparability in the presentation of the results of these studies. In Chapter 7, therefore, we present a suggested schema for comparing program success and costs. Finally, we present a summary outline of the procedural steps which we have discussed in earlier chapters.

We feel that readers can best use this primer if, in conjunction, they examine several of the studies cited in the bibliography. These studies were selected because they appeared to us to be better than average impact evaluations. We suggest that if special attention is given to their treatment of topics discussed in this primer, when any deficiencies have been corrected, the reader can use these studies as models for his own measurements of program impact. Thus we hope that this primer together with the bibliography will serve as a jumping off point in the evaluative process, permitting evaluators to develop their own analyses without committing the same mistakes as occurred in earlier studies.

2

MANPOWER PROGRAM OBJECTIVES AND OPERATIONAL CRITERIA OF PROGRAM SUCCESS

There are four parties who may benefit from manpower programs. These are society as a whole, participants in the program, employers, and the government. And, under some circumstances, trade unions may also be vitally affected by manpower programs. Each of these groups has different outcomes which they wish the manpower programs to accomplish. Therefore, depending on the perspective taken, the objectives of manpower programs will differ. From a societal point of view, the goals of manpower programs are put in terms of aggregate changes, for example increased aggregate production, improved equity in the overall distribution of income and employment, and reductions in the national unemployment rate. For the individual participant the goals are more limited, usually to benefits which directly affect him, such as improvement in his earnings and increases in his satisfaction. An employer, too, will tend to look at the programs in terms of his own interests. For instance, he will be concerned with how the productivity of his labor force has been increased. Finally, the government will view the programs in terms of the various societal objectives, but, in addition, will seek programs which will aid its budgetary position.

Obviously, there is a great deal of overlap between the goals[1] of the four groups. The government acts as the agent of society in operating the programs. As such, definitions of program success will naturally coincide in most areas for the government and for society. Similarly, individuals and employers as members of society are interested in aggregate changes as well as those directly affecting them. Likewise, the effect of programs on individuals will determine in part their success in terms of society. Increased employment of participants in programs is likely to improve aggregate employment, and improvement in the production of individual firms may lead to increased aggregate production.

There may also be an overlap between the goals for each of the parties. For instance, the reduction in an individual's unemployment may increase his earnings as well as decrease his feeling of dependency. Since the effects, however, may have independent importance for the individual, we believe that all should be considered.

There also may be conflicts, however, between the goals of the different parties and between various goals for a particular party. Thus we may find that a program which improves the income of the participants is very costly to the government or that a program which is highly efficient at increasing aggregate production leads to greater inequity in the national distribution of income. These conflicts in possible program achievement raise the problem of ranking the objectives of each of the parties. While on a theoretical level one can argue that societal objectives should be paramount, the evaluator must be a realist. He should recognize that the rewards and costs of manpower programs to particular interested parties who have political influence may play an important role in determining the size, scope, and even the existence of the program. He must then take account of the goals of all four parties.

Furthermore, it is necessary for the manpower program evaluator to present data on many program objectives so that the different parties will have the data necessary for them to evaluate the

---

[1] "Goals" and "objectives" are used interchangeably in this discussion.

program. Ideally, the users of manpower program evaluations should specify those goals which they believe to be the most important. The evaluator and users would consult each other to ensure that the evaluation measured the most meaningful objectives. Unfortunately, the evaluator seldom has the opportunity to discuss the needs of the users of his reports. In addition, the relative ranking of the goals may change over time. Thus we suggest that the evaluator examine as many objectives as he can in his study.

To facilitate the choice of objectives to be studied, we present a list of goals for society, the individual, employers, and the government. We feel that *all* manpower programs can be judged to a large extent in terms of these objectives. We realize, however, that each program will have a different method of reaching these objectives and will put somewhat different emphasis on each of the goals. The list is, of course, not all-inclusive. It should, however, provide many of the most important goals of manpower programs. Below each goal we present specific operational criteria to measure the success of a manpower program in meeting the objective.

This list does not assign priorities to specific goals; we believe that assignment of priorities is the ultimate responsibility of the decisionmaker. We do feel, however, that certain items should be given more attention than others on strictly methodological grounds. Because economic criteria are much better defined at this time than are some of the other criteria, we suggest that these measurements will be easier to make, and will be relatively unambiguous. The list has been ordered accordingly. For each of the possible users two types of objectives have been presented. The first group includes goals where operational criteria exist and are presently being used for evaluation purposes. The second set of goals are included with the hope that further development of operational measures will be stimulated.

Finally, it is assumed that the goals will be measured after participation in the program. Some, however, could be applied equally as well during the program. For example, training allowances may lead to greater personal incomes for the program participants. For simplicity, all gains which occur after the program have been classified as benefits and those which occur during the program as negative costs.

I. Manpower Program Objectives for Society

A. *Objectives with Clear Operational Criteria*
1. *Improved Equity in the Distribution of Income and Employment, Especially for Target Groups*[2]
   a. *Increased Incomes.* The increase in the earnings of target group members relative to the average change in income for all workers
   b. *Increased Employment.* The increase in the percent of time that all target group members are employed and the decrease in the percent of time they are unemployed after the program, relative to the change in the averages for all workers. A less useful measure because of seasonality and time trends would be the increase in the percent of target group members who are employed at given times relative to the national averages.
2. *Increased National Production.* The increase in the gross national product (GNP) which should approximate the sum of the changes in earnings of all persons affected by the programs, including persons who are not program participants
3. *Reduced Unemployment.* The decline in the average percent of time persons affected by the program are unemployed after the program. A less useful measure because of seasonality and time trend would be the change in the percent of these persons who are unemployed at given times.
4. *Increased Social Satisfaction*
   a. *Increased Satisfaction with Social Institutions and Increased Social Participation.* The increase in the number of persons who are affected by manpower

---

[2] Groups which might be considered are:
a. Persons defined as poor.
b. Members of minorities (Negroes, American Indians, persons with Spanish surnames).
c. The handicapped (physically handicapped, mentally retarded, mentally ill, alcoholics).
d. Groups with high unemployment rates (teenagers, aged, exconvicts, school dropouts).
e. Groups receiving government benefits (welfare recipients, unemployment insurance claimants, veterans).
f. Others (heads of households, farmers, persons in depressed areas, the unemployed, and underemployed).

programs who participate in political activities. The increase in the average score on scales of attitudes and alienation toward social institutions, e.g. schools, police, politics, and welfare agencies

   b. *Increased Job Satisfaction.* The improvement in average scores on job satisfaction scales

   c. *Increased Overall Satisfaction.* The increase in average scores on social indicators

B. *Objectives More Difficult to Measure*[3]

   1. *Stable Prices.* The stability in wages and prices in those industries and occupations in which persons affected by the program are employed relative to average changes for all wages and prices. Special attention should be given to "bottleneck" industries and occupations.

   2. *Reduced Asocial Behavior.* The reduction among persons affected by the program who are arrested and convicted of crimes, who participate in riots, or who are involved in other socially unacceptable activities. Reduced recidivism rate and parole revocations for former inmates of correctional institutions might also be utilized.

   3. *Reduced Dependency on Government.* The reduction in the number of persons who receive welfare and unemployment insurance, the amount received of each, and the proportion of time these are received. Psychological scales of dependency might also be used to examine the degree of dependency as perceived by persons whom the program affects.

   4. *Increased Voluntary Leisure.* The reduction in the number of hours worked to conform with individuals' desires. A second measure would be the reduction in the proportion of persons affected by the program who work more than they desire. Finally, the improvement in scores on an attitude scale measuring satisfaction with leisure might be examined.

   5. *Improved Family Life.* The reduction in the proportion of program-affected persons who become divorced, desert, or are deserted largely because of economic

---

[3] We present these objectives because we believe that they should ultimately be considered in evaluations of manpower programs. Presently, operational criteria are lacking. We suggest some possibilities but further definitional work is necessary.

reasons. Changes in attitudes toward other family members should also be examined.
6. *Improved Race Relations.* The proportion of persons affected by the program who improve their attitudes and behavior toward members of other races
7. *Improved Health.* The average improvement in the nutritional level as measured by changes in the amount spent on food and protein content. The effect on health can be measured by the reduction in average number of days sick, the proportion of program involved persons with emotional problems, and the value of health services provided to program participants.
8. *Improved Housing.* The average improvement in the quality of housing based on the Census definitions

II. Manpower Program Objectives for Individuals

A. *Objectives with Clear Operational Criteria*
1. *Increased Incomes.* The average increase in the incomes of program participants with different characteristics. The income increase could be from either increased employment or higher levels of productivity.
2. *Reduced Unemployment.* The reduction in the average percent of the time after the program that different types of program participants are unemployed. A less useful measure because of seasonality and time trends would be the reduction in the percent of different types of participants who are unemployed at a given time.
3. *Increased Satisfaction*
   a. *Increased Satisfaction with Work.* The average improvement in scores on job satisfaction tests by different types of program participants
   b. *Increased Satisfaction with General Conditions.* The increase in average scores on social indicators by different types of participants
   c. *Increased Satisfaction with Social Status.* The improvement in social and occupational status of participants with differing characteristics as measured by the Duncan Scale or Warner Social-Economic Status Index

B. *Objectives More Difficult to Measure*
  1. *Increased Voluntary Leisure*. The increase in the average number of hours when work is not sought or desired at the going wage for different groups of persons affected by the program. A second measure would be the reduction in the proportion of the groups who work more than they desire.
  2. *Reduced Dependency*. The reduced proportion of different participant groups who receive welfare and unemployment insurance and the reduction in the amount received of each. The reduction in the degree of dependency as perceived by each group, should also be examined. Scales of dependency might be used for the last.
  3. *Improved Health*. The average improvement in the nutritional level of different types of participants as measured by changes in the amount spent on food and protein content in the diet. The effect on health can be measured by reductions in the average number of days sick, the proportion with emotional problems, and the value of health services provided for different groups of program participants.
  4. *Improved Family Life*. The reduction in the proportion of program-affected persons who become divorced, desert, or are deserted largely because of economic reasons. Changes in attitudes toward other family members should also be examined.
  5. *Improved Housing*. The average increase in quality of housing, based on the Census definitions, of program participants with different characteristics

III. Manpower Program Objectives for Employers

A. *Objectives with Clear Operational Criteria*
  1. *Jobs of Specific Employers Filled*. The proportion of participants accepting jobs in "bottleneck" industries, in occupations where workers are in short supply, and with particular employers. The number of vacancies and public-employment service jobs orders filled, by industry and occupation, are a second measure.
  2. *Jobs in Particular Areas Filled*. The number and pro-

portion of the participants who live in labor shortage and in depressed areas. Reduction in the number and the length of vacancies and unfilled job orders in employment service offices in each of these areas

B. *Objective More Difficult to Measure: Improved Productivity of Particular Employers' Labor Forces.* The increase in average output per manhour of firms affected by manpower programs. These might be shown by the improvement in the average level of achievement on work sampling tests for the employers' work forces. Also the change in the years of school completed and changes in their knowledge level as measured by achievement tests (such as Armed Forces entrance examination, Metropolitan, Stanford, and Wide Range tests) should be examined for the work forces of specific employees.

IV. Manpower Program Objectives for Government Operations

A. *Reduced Costs of Government Operations.* The reduction in the proportion of persons affected by the program who receive welfare or unemployment insurance or who need to use the services of the employment service after the programs. Also to be measured is the reduction in the average time spent providing services to these persons by each of the agencies involved and the cost of these services.

B. *Reduced Transfer Payments.* The reduced average amount of unemployment insurance and public assistance received by the program participants. Changes in public assistance paid to other family members should also be measured.

C. *Increased Tax Revenues through an Increased Tax Base.* The increase in the taxes paid by persons involved with the program. Separate calculations should be made for federal personal income, excise, and social security taxes. Local and state tax measurements should include income, sales, and real estate taxes.

D. *Increased Number of Persons Available for Military Service or Other Public Service.* The increase in draft-age youth who are reclassified as acceptable for military service, Peace Corps, VISTA, or similar types of public service

3

MEASURING THE SUCCESS OF MANPOWER PROGRAMS

Because benefits of manpower programs may be received by society, by individuals, by employers, and by the government, and because each has somewhat different goals and criteria of success, separate calculations of program benefits are required for each of these groups on the basis of the benefits as defined for that group. The methodology for each calculation will be approximately the same for all of the groups, however. Each group seeks to determine the differences which exist in a set of measures, with and without the manpower programs. This will require a comparison between the experience, behavior, and attitudes of program participants after participating in the program and those expected if they had not participated.

The Choice of a Control Group

Since it is impossible to measure after an event what would have happened if the event did not occur, the evaluation must usually rely on the use of control groups whose experience, behavior, and attitudes after the program correspond to those which the program participants would have had if they had not entered the program.

Random Control Groups. One method appears most likely to select a control group which will accurately reflect the expected behavior of the program participants.[1] All of the persons who are qualified to enter the program must be contacted immediately before the start of the program to find out who are still interested in entering it. The group still wishing to be considered would then be split randomly with only one group assigned to actually enter the program. The second group would be given the regular services, if any, normally available to them. If this method would yield too small an experimental or control group possessing a particular characteristic, the group wishing to enter the program should be stratified by this characteristic. Then differing sampling proportions would be used from each of the sampling units. The sampling from each unit, however, would be random.

If the evaluation seeks only to determine which of several alternative programs is preferable, a variation on this procedure would be used. A control group that does not enter any of the programs would not be necessary. Recruitment would not exceed the number of program slots and persons qualified and interested in participating would be randomly assigned to the programs. Persons in each program would serve as control group members for comparison with the participants in other programs.[2]

Such procedures have the outstanding advantage that they are statistically sound. Known probabilities can be given to chance differences in the success of the two groups. This would not be true of other means for selecting control groups.

Problems of Random Selection. Several problems are involved in the random selection of a control group. The first is the reluctance of the operating agencies to exclude fully qualified persons from receiving the services of the agencies. Such an

---

[1] Even using this procedure, however, when programs are large relative to the universe of need, the success of the experimental group may have an effect on the control group. This is discussed in more detail below.

[2] It should be understood, however, that this procedure where no control group is used will not be applicable if benefits per unit of cost is the desired goal unless the costs are the same for all programs. This is explained in Robert S. Goldfarb, "The Evaluation of Government Programs: The Case of New Haven's Manpower Training Activities," a report to the Manpower Administration, 1968, pp. 200-201.

exclusion is felt by the program operators to be analogous to a doctor's not treating a patient who has a disease when a drug is available. If the analogy is carried further, however, in medicine we demand that drugs be tested before they are administered so that their effects are known. This testing is done through just the process recommended here. Persons with the disease are divided randomly. One group receives the drug and the other group receives placebos. This is the only scientific manner to test the actual effects of the drug. In medicine, it is recognized that it could be much more disastrous to administer a drug which has no effects or dangerous side effects because of an untested belief that the drug is beneficial, than to properly test the drug and if it is ineffective substitute a better alternative. The same can be said about manpower programs.

On strictly practical grounds there are seldom enough positions in a manpower program to satisfy the universe of need. Almost always there is a rationing of program openings. Ideally the positions will be assigned to those most needing the program services. Usually, however, assignment is on the basis of some other, less beneficial criterion, such as on a first come first served basis for those who qualify for the program, or to those most likely to succeed in the program ("creaming"). The random assignment technique will not reduce the amount of services provided nor the eligibility of the participants. It will merely change which qualified people receive the services and may more equitably distribute the benefits of the program.

Another problem with the random selection technique is that it requires more extensive selection than would normally occur. Under ordinary conditions it is only necessary to interview, test, and refer persons to the program until all slots are filled. With the random selection technique, enough additional persons must be found who also qualify so that a control group of adequate size can be selected. Since, however, the projects selected for evaluation will form only a very small part of each manpower program the increase in cost will be relatively small. It should be viewed as a cost of the research which will be well repaid in terms of the accuracy of the results.

If the control group and the experimental group are identified at the start of the project, efforts can be made to keep track of these persons. This will improve the response rate for the evaluation and reduce the costs of followup. The choice of retrospective control groups usually involves trying to contact persons with whom there has been no link for many months. Many cannot be located and a great deal of time and effort is spent trying to locate the others. Thus, the use of the random selection technique may lead to a lower total cost for the evaluation.

Finally, the random selection technique requires a longer time period from the start to the end of the evaluation than would a retrospective study. However, in terms of a new program or a changing program the random selection technique will present its findings at least as quickly as will a retrospective study.

Other types of control groups. The random selection technique requires that the evaluation be built into the program planning. In some situations (though few) this is not possible. In these circumstances, retrospective studies may be the only alternative and a biased control group will have to be used. Naturally, the less biased the control group the more reliance which can be placed on the results of the evaluation. Unfortunately, it is impossible to say with any degree of certainty which nonrandomly selected group has the least bias. Of the possible control groups, the group which probably comes closest to approximating the program participants are those who qualified for but did not enter the program. At least they, like the program participants, showed an interest in the program and were able to meet the program's entrance requirements.

They were, of course, unlike the participants in that they did not enter the program, and the reasons for this lead to a bias in comparing them to the program participants. (To the extent that these factors can be identified, they should be included as independent variables in the analysis). Persons who do not enter manpower programs may be either those persons who feel that they can do better on their own or those who feel they cannot succeed in the program. The first group would probably be expected to have a better future than the program participants and the second group would have a bleaker outlook than the participants. A second source of bias is selection by the agency. If funds are inadequate to handle all applicants, the least qualified or least needy may be excluded from the program. Again, these individuals would not be fully comparable to the program participants: the former would be less able and the latter would be better able than the participants to find employment on their own.[3]

Selection of persons who have not applied for the program to serve as a control group suffers from the same problems. Examples of such control groups would be random samples from among the unemployed, from among the applicants to the employment service, from among the poor, or from among some similar group. A major indication of the disparity between these groups and program participants lies in the basic question: "Why did these persons not participate in the program?" The answer might be lack of interest, lack of need, lack of ability or another reason for self-selection, or the refusal of the sponsoring agency to enroll them because of ineligibility or inability. All of these reasons would cause the control group to have different patterns of behavior and attitudes from those expected of the program participants.[4]

Probably the least desirable control group arrangement is to use before and after comparisons of the program participants' experience, even when changes in the average levels of employment and earnings for the labor force are relied on to deflate the changes of the participants. Program participants are not average members of the labor force. Typically, average members of the labor force are not even eligible for program participation. Thus to compare the experiences of target groups such as teenage Negroes from poor families with national or local statistics for the total labor force is obviously incorrect.[5] Moreover, individuals who have high unemployment rates in one period may be expected to have high unemployment rates later, but they will usually have greater than average increases in employment. This is particularly true of youths and reentrants to the labor force.

The use of any of these control groups in retrospective studies is definitely an inferior choice for another reason, also. In addition to the problems of noncomparability, they also must rely on existing records from which to draw a sample. To the extent that these

---

[3] This type of control group is used and discussed in Michael E. Borus, *The Economic Effectiveness of Retraining the Unemployed,* Boston: Federal Reserve Bank of Boston, 1966.

[4] Control groups of this type are presented in Gerald G. Somers, editor, *Retraining the Unemployed,* Madison: University of Wisconsin Press, 1968.

[5] This procedure is used in U. S. Department of Labor, *The Influence of MDTA Training on Earnings,* Manpower Evaluation Report Number 8, Washington: Manpower Administration, 1968.

lists are incomplete or inaccurate, further biases may be introduced.

In summary, nonrandom control groups should be avoided wherever possible since it is impossible to be certain of the results of such evaluations. Certainty can only be achieved when the operating system has a technique for random selection of control groups built into it. The writers recognize, however, that more research is warranted in this area to improve the quality of evaluations under less satisfactory conditions. Further research would be extremely useful to measure the relative merits of each of the control groups discussed.

Sources of Data on Control Group Members. When retrospective studies are made and require the use of existing records to identify persons to serve as members of control groups, the evaluator may turn to several sources of data. If he desires to identify individuals who applied for a program but who did not enter it (the preferred control group for retrospective studies), he must rely on records which may exist in the local office of the employment service (either in special program files or as written comments on individuals' Form ES-511) or in other agencies dealing with manpower programs.[6] The use of such records, however, requires the identification of the projects to be studied, the contacting of the local offices, a detailed search of their records to ensure a complete list, and then the selection of a sample from this list. Since these records probably will not contain any information on the individuals after the completion of the programs, the individuals will have to be contacted or the national records checked to make certain that none of the control group subsequently participated in the program. These procedures will be both costly and time consuming.

Alternatively, control groups may be constructed from among

---

[6] The USTES began experimental operation of an electronic record system in July 1969. The system, known as ESARS, will provide records of the demographic characteristics for each applicant to the employment service office. Demographic characteristics will include: year of birth, sex, education, labor force status, weeks unemployed in the last year, ethnic status, veteran, family size, family income classification, previous manpower programs participated in, whether handicapped, whether an unemployment insurance claimant, office location, and social security number. Also included in the system will be a record of each of the services performed for the individual. When this system becomes operative on a large scale, the central tapes should be able to provide information on all persons who were referred to a program but who did not enter it, as well as all ES services performed for program participants.

individuals similar to the participants who have been surveyed in other studies. Several other studies of this type exist.

Current Population Survey. The Current Population Survey (CPS) interviews approximately 50,000 households each month and approximately 187,500 each year. Each household averages more than two individuals over age thirteen. Thus data are collected for more than 100,000 people each month. For each of these persons information is collected on a Control Card CPO-260, including: sex, age, color, marital status, educational attainment, relation to household head, veteran's status, number of family members, family income category for the preceding 12 months, occupation, industry, location, description of housing, and social security number. There is also an address and telephone number. With these data a closely matched control group could be constructed for subsequent contact.

If data are desired on the earnings and income of these individuals and their work experience during the previous calendar year, special surveys are conducted in February, March, and April of each year to gather this information. Approximately 50,000 households are asked both earnings and work experience questions which allows the integration of the two sets of data.

Two problems are involved in the use of these data. First, to eliminate the persons who have participated in the program under study, the social security numbers of the possible CPS survey control group members would have to be compared with the national listings for the program. Technically, this would not be difficult.

The second problem involves the question of sample size. It might not be possible to secure a large control group where matching is desired on many characteristics. Likewise, it will be difficult to construct large samples to match groups who comprise a small portion of the population. This problem takes on major proportions where matching on the basis of the individual's work experience is needed (as it will be for most manpower programs since they deal primarily with the unemployed) and where the CPS earnings and employment data are also to be used for dependent variables. The work experience questions are asked in February and April and the earnings questions are asked in March. Thus data on these variables for the preceding year (year $T-1$) is available for approximately 50,000 households. If, however, the dependent variable is data for the following year (year T), data can only be secured for the 25,000 households who are in the CPS sample for the second time (in year T+1). Furthermore, since persons unemployed in a year constitute only a small proportion of the noninstitutional population 16 years old or over (13 percent in 1966 and 1967), subgroups may be difficult to find.[7] The existence of such problems can be found by comparing the size of particular subgroups in the CPS with the minimum number of control group members required. Because of its large size, however, the CPS should provide the necessary control group in most cases when fine breakdowns are not necessary or when the individuals are to be contacted directly. Therefore, it appears to be the most useful existing source of control groups for retrospective studies, especially when it can be supplemented by other surveys.

Urban Employment Survey. The Urban Employment Survey (UES) was begun in June 1968. Approximately 1800 different households are interviewed each month. These households are in the Concentrated Employment Program areas in six cities: Atlanta, Chicago, Detroit, Houston, Los Angeles, and New York. Approximately the same information on demographic characteristics is gathered for each household member on the UES-1 as is gathered in the CPS. In addition, the UES-3 asks household members about their earnings and income during the last 12 months, their first job after leaving school, their training, their major occupation, their mobility, the means of transportation they use to get to employment, and their job satisfaction.

This survey has the advantages of: (1) sampling primarily from the poor for whom most manpower programs are concerned, and (2) asking specifically about participation in training programs. The latter allows removal of potential control group members who were program participants without having to compare their social security numbers with the national program tapes. The value of this source of data may be limited, however, by its relatively small size and its use in only six cities. Its major value at this time would probably be to supplement the samples gathered by the CPS in those cities.

---

[7] A possible way to get around this problem is to get social security earnings data on all persons in the 50,000 households for the previous year (year T−1). Matching can then be made on this variable and the sample size will be twice as large since there will not be the need to consider only the reinterview portion of the sample.

National Longitudinal Survey. Four groups of five thousand individuals are being sampled annually between 1966-68 and 1971-73. The four groups are males between 14 and 24 when first interviewed, females in the same age group, women initially between 30 and 45, and men 45 to 59 at the first interview. The sample is stratified nationally and there is a three to one over-sampling of nonwhites. The surveys collect the following information about each respondent: age, sex, race, marital status, number of dependents, family income, education and training, work experience, earnings and income of the individual and his spouse during the preceding 12 months, current labor force status, health, assets, family background, mobility, and social security number. Much additional information is also secured, so that there is a great deal of data about each of these subgroups.

There are also problems in using these data to select control groups. They can only be used for the sex and age groups they include. Second, even for these groups there may not be enough sample members in small categories of the population. Next, if the dependent variables are to be taken from the survey, the periods of work experience and earnings for the program participants must be the same as for the control group. The data in the Longitudinal Surveys are collected only once a year (in October for the male teenagers, February for the female teenagers, and in June for the older men and women).[8] Thus to be comparable the program participants must also be interviewed in these months. This would not be a problem if the control group members were to be contacted. Finally, the social security numbers of the potential control group members would have to be checked against the national lists to remove those persons who had participated in the programs.

Area Labor Survey. Beginning in January 1966 the Bureau of Employment Security contracted to supplement the CPS sample in Pittsburgh, Cleveland, and Detroit. Each month approximately 310, 375, and 150 different households were interviewed in the three cities, respectively. In January 1967, 300 central-city families per month were added to the surveys in Cleveland. One hundred and fifty families from the central-city in Chicago and 300 families in the Philadelphia central-city were also added at that time. The Area Labor Survey was completed at the end of calendar 1968,

---

[8] The times for data collection after 1968 may be changed for the older workers.

and interviewing in Detroit only occurred in 1966 and 1967. Consequently, its use for control group comparisons is limited to the short period and the cities where interviewing took place.

Survey of Economic Opportunity. In January through March of 1966 approximately 30,000 households were interviewed in a survey conducted by the Office of Economic Opportunity. The sample was made up of approximately 18,000 households stratified to give a representation of the total population and 12,000 low-income households. Data were secured from those households for 1965. The same addresses were visited one year later and approximately 24,000 of the households were available for re-interview. An additional 6000 households were added mainly from new construction. Information for calendar 1966 was secured at that time.

In 1966, information for each individual in the family was gathered on: social security number, age, sex, race, veteran and school status, education, work experience, earnings, previous training and its uses, and migration. Information was also gathered on family assets and liabilities, family income and housing characteristics. In 1967 data were gathered on approximately the same variables, plus health, marital status, and child bearing.[9]

For programs operating in 1965 and 1966, these data should be very useful. The survey includes a large number of persons who would be eligible for manpower programs, and data on key variables are provided to match them with the program participants. Information is also provided on many of the important criteria of success for manpower programs. Its usefulness, however, will be limited to comparisons with 1965 and 1966 program participants; for the individuals' characteristics and situations are known only for these years. It is possible that cyclical or other changes in subsequent years would make them noncomparable to later program participants. Moreover, it would be necessary to eliminate from the group those persons who subsequently were in manpower programs if their experience in years after 1966 were to be used for control purposes. This could be done by comparing social security numbers with those on the program tapes listing participants.

Social Security Administration data. The Social Security Ad-

---

[9] A detailed description of the survey is available from the Office of Economic Opportunity, "1967 Survey of Economic Opportunity Codebook."

ministration maintains a special file called the Continuous Work History Sample (CWHS), providing a 1 percent sample of the individuals who have applied for social security numbers. Information available for these persons includes: age, sex, race, prior annual covered earnings and quarters with covered employment, and employer industry and location.

The use of these data to form control groups involves several problems. First, the CWHS tapes do not contain identification of individuals although they permit linkage with tapes from SSA through common case numbers. Some form of accommodation would have to be worked out with the Social Security Administration if social security numbers are to be run against the national lists of program participants to make sure that the individuals in the potential control group have not been program participants too.

Also, since the CWHS contains only a limited set of information, matching on these variables may not be sufficient to select a truly comparable group. Important variables such as education, marital status, health, existence of other forms of training, and family income are absent. It would be impossible to secure this information directly since the individual's address is not a part of the record. This also means that the only dependent variables which could be examined using this source of a control group are the information on earnings, number of quarters of covered employment, and industry and location of employer. While earnings is a key measure of the success of manpower programs, the shortcomings of the social security data would appear to severely limit its usefulness as a source of control groups. As will be discussed below, however, social security records are the best source of earnings data for long term follow-ups of control groups selected from other sources.

The Choice of an Experimental Group

Manpower program evaluations should measure the effects on all persons affected by the program. Included should be the effects on all program participants, members of the participants' families, other persons with whom the participants work, and other groups who may be affected.

The Inclusion of All Program Participants. Evaluations of a program should measure the effects of that program upon all participants; the effects upon dropouts as well as persons who complete the courses. Dropouts from a program may be benefited by a program even though they do not remain until its end. They may change their attitudes or improve some of their skills while they are in the program. Alternatively, these individuals may suffer by being in a program; they may miss job opportunities during the period they are in the course or they may be labeled as failures for not having completed the program. In either case the dropout is affected by the program and the effects should be included in the evaluation.

Likewise, the evaluation should measure the effects of the manpower programs on all of those who complete the program, not only on those who are placed because of it or who make use of it. Beneficial or negative changes in attitudes may occur among program participants even if they do not appear to be affected in their employment. Thus the effects of the program on all participants must be measured if a full accounting is to be achieved. This does not mean that no distinctions should be made between different types of program participants. The analysis should seek to determine the differences which exist between completers and dropouts in order to determine the necessity of reducing the proportion of dropouts or the possibility of shortening courses.

Other Family Members. Similarly, evaluations should measure the effects of the program on other members of the participants' families. Changes which may occur in the earnings, employment, attitudes, and status of the participants are very likely to affect other members of their families as well. Most likely to change will be the labor force participation rates and the attitudes toward work and education of the other family members. Again, in order to achieve a complete accounting for the project these secondary effects should be measured.

Other Groups for Whom Measurement Is Necessary.[10] An attempt should be made to measure the effects of programs on other workers who are completely unrelated to the program. Four groups of workers can be identified who might be affected by manpower programs.

First, it is possible that program participants merely displace persons who held or who would hold the same jobs as those in

---

[10] Further discussion of these points may be found in Einar Hardin and Michael E. Borus, "An Economic Evaluation of the Retraining Program in Michigan: Methodological Problems of Research," *Proceedings of the Social Statistics Section,* American Statistical Association, 1966, pp. 133-37.

which participants are placed. This may result in displacement of average workers by the poor or some other group for whom it is socially desirable to increase their earnings and employment. (An example of this kind of program would be the training of minority group youth to enter apprenticeship programs which have a limited number of openings.) Such displacement could be justified on equity grounds, although it means that there is no increase in aggregate efficiency. It may be, however, that the manpower programs replace one group of marginal workers with a similar group, so that there is no gain using either efficiency or equity criteria.

There may also be displacement of workers in other industries than that for which the manpower program is designed. Most manpower programs do not create a demand for the services of participants. Rather, they must assume a given distribution of a fixed level of demand, which dictates job openings.[11] Under this assumption, however, an increase in the supply of labor in a certain occupation would lower the wage rate, would increase the supply of goods to meet orders which could not previously be filled because of a shortage of labor, or would cause displacement. The first two possibilities would increase employment in the occupation and the production of goods which are produced by that occupation. If, however, the aggregate level of demand is fixed there would be reductions in the demand for the goods produced by workers in other occupations. This would mean a reduction in the earnings and possibly in the employment of persons in these occupations.[12] These effects should also be measured.

---

[11] Presumably government fiscal and monetary policy are designed to achieve full employment regardless of whether a particular manpower program is implemented. At the same time, however, manpower programs which increase the employability of the labor force and thus reduce manpower bottlenecks will allow full employment at lower levels of price increase. This consideration would be of special importance if monetary and fiscal policy were restricted to less than full employment levels because of inflationary problems. Measures of these effects need also be developed. For a more complete discussion see Gosta Rehn, "Summary and Comments on a Benefit/Cost Study of Adult Retraining in Sweden," a working paper prepared for the Manpower and Social Affairs Directorate, Organization for Economic Cooperation and Development, Paris, 1969, mimeograph.

[12] For example, if I want to purchase orange juice but the price is too high or I will have to wait too long for it to arrive, I instead buy milk. When, however, the price of orange juice falls or it becomes more generally available because of a manpower program to increase the number of orange pickers, I will shift my demand and buy the orange juice. This shift in demand allows the employment of more persons and greater income for the

Third, in situations where there is unemployment the effect of a manpower program may be to increase aggregate earnings and employment by a greater amount than the increases for the individual program participants because unemployed persons take the jobs the program participants would have had if they had not entered the program. The individual program participant gains to the extent that his new job is better than the job he would have had. His gain is the income and employment on his new job minus what he would have received, if he had remained on his old job. Society, however, need not subtract the earnings from the job the program participant leaves if someone else from among the unemployed becomes employed in that job. Society receives increased production equal to the total product of the program participant, not only his personal gain. This situation is based, however, on the assumption that the new job of the program participant would not otherwise be filled, i.e. that there would not be displacement, and that aggregate demand is increased.

Finally, there may also be social gains in excess of private gains even if there is no unemployment, when the placement of the program participant leads to others being hired also. Technology is such that in some industries jobs are complementary. If one job is vacant, other jobs which are dependent upon it cannot be filled. For example, a shortage of computer programmers will limit the use of computers and the need for keypunch operators. In these cases, the improvement in the earnings and employment of the program participant (who becomes a computer operator in the example) understates the benefits which society receives. To the extent that the now necessary other workers (keypunch operators) earn or are employed more than they would have been, these too are benefits resulting from the program.

The effects of manpower programs on these four groups of individuals may completely outweigh the direct effects upon the program participants. Therefore, every evaluation should attempt to identify the characteristics of persons who are displaced or hired because of placement of the program participants. Then these persons should be compared with a control group to determine the effects of the program on them too. Unfortunately, measure-

---

orange industry. It hurts the dairy farmers and processors, however; it lowers their revenues and possibly their production and employment. If we measure the effect of manpower programs solely in terms of the orange industry we may be missing some of the secondary effects.

ments of these possible effects on secondary groups have not been well developed and further methodological studies are needed.

The Use of Multivariate Analysis

To conduct an evaluation of manpower programs it is necessary to measure the relationships between the program goals (the dependent variables) and a variety of independent variables including the personal characteristics of participants, the program components, and the conditions under which the programs operate. It will be the job of the evaluation to discover which of these independent variables are important and the nature of the relationship. However, most dependent variables with which evaluations of manpower programs deal, are functions of more than one independent variable. Under these circumstances the analyses should treat simultaneously all of the independent variables which are believed to be relevant. To omit some variables in the analysis may lead to distorted conclusions due to correlation or interaction among these variables and those independent variables which are included in the anaylsis.[13] Therefore, multivariate techniques should be used in the evaluations to discover and test the statistical significance of any relationships which are observed.[14]

The use of simple cross tabulations to isolate such relationships will be inadequate in most cases. For instance, the effects of race, age, education, and skill level on earnings are all interrelated. Yet each of the effects should be distinguished. To cross tabulate by all of these variables would involve so many cells that the sample would have to be enormous. In addition, the tables would be so large as to be unmanageable. Multiple regression and correlation techniques, on the other hand, require a much smaller sample size and permit easy interpretation of the findings.

Some of the independent variables which should be examined are described below.

Personal Independent Variables. Manpower evaluations should examine the effects of the manpower programs on groups of participants for two reasons. First, the analyses should determine whether a particular program will benefit certain target groups for

---

[13] For a brief discussion of this problem see Daniel Suits, *Statistics: An Introduction to Quantitative Economic Research,* Chicago: Rand McNally & Company, 1963, pp. 109-115.

[14] Chi-square tests would be appropriate for categorically defined dependent variables.

whom the programs are designed and to find which programs serve the groups best. Independent variables should be included in the analysis to represent different groups of the poor and the unemployed, such as: Negroes, Mexican-Americans, Indians, the handicapped, teenagers, the aged, school dropouts, exconvicts, welfare and unemployment insurance recipients, and veterans.

It is also necessary to treat personal characteristics in the evaluation in order to improve the efficiency of the programs. Programs will have varying results for different types of people. Once it is known which individuals get the greatest benefits from each program then those individuals can be assigned so that the success of each program is maximized. This objective may be in conflict with the desire to benefit target groups if these groups receive lower benefits from all of the programs than do other workers. If it is still desired to have target group participation, as would seem likely, it will be more efficient to allocate the target groups to those programs where they receive the largest benefits. Then if there are still program slots, the individuals who would have the greatest expected benefits would be enrolled.

Degree of success should be measured for such characteristics of the program participants as: age, sex, race, ethnic groups, number of dependents, family size, education, curriculum, handicaps, health, assets, family income, past earnings, employment, mobility and turnover, employment status before enrollment, welfare and unemployment compensation status, existence of previous training, skill level, occupation, military status, attitudes toward work, attitudes toward society, police record, intelligence, and aptitudes.

Program Component Independent Variables. Most manpower programs consist of a set of activities and many of these are common to several programs. It would be extremely useful in modifying existing programs and in the planning of new programs to know for present programs which of the program components are most effective for various types of participants. It would also be desirable to have information on the most effective combinations of components. To the extent that the length and nature of the components supplied to individuals differ within or between the programs, multivariate techniques can be used to identify effective components. Therefore, the evaluations should examine programs which include a variety of components and where the length of the components and the program vary, and should include as independent variables the amount of each of these services performed in a program (this will usually be expressed in terms of hours spent per participant) and, if possible, a measure of quality.

The range of possible activities suitable to aid a person in securing employment is almost limitless. Some of the components of present manpower programs which should be considered for inclusion in manpower evaluations are listed in the table on page 46.

Exogenous Independent Variables. Manpower programs will also differ in their effectiveness depending on the conditions under which they operate. Possible factors affecting program success include: the level of unemployment, growth in employment, the average earnings, and the degree of manufacturing in both the area in which the program occurs and nationally. The size and nature (farm, rural, depressed, etc.) of the area in which the program occurs, and the degree of discrimination in the area might also be included. If the program involves training for specific skills, the type of skill, the demand for workers with the given skill, and the average earnings of persons with that skill would be important. These variables should be included in the analysis as independent variables to determine under what conditions the programs are most effective and which programs are most effective under particular conditions.

Determining Proper Program Size—Measuring at the Margin

A basic question which the evaluation should answer is, "What should be the program's size?" (including the possibility that the answer may be that no program is justified). Ideally, the evaluation would provide an accounting of the total benefits derived from the program at each possible level of program activity. The decisionmaker could then compare programs and allocate his expenditures to yield the level of activity for each which would maximize the total return on the total expenditure. To do this, he would allocate his resources so that each additional dollar was spent on the program which yielded the greatest return for that dollar, given the distribution of previous expenditures.

To date, however, evaluations of manpower programs have not presented these data. Rather, average benefits have been calculated for a program at fixed levels of program activity. In order to make program size decisions, users of these analyses have had to assume that the average benefits of different programs have a direct relationship to the benefits at the margin, i.e. that adding a person to a program with a high average benefit will be more beneficial than enrolling the person in a program with a lower average benefit. Only if this assumption is true, however, will the decision-maker end up with the optimal allocation of his resources.

There are techniques, however, which can be used to roughly approximate the effects of changes in program size. One technique is to relate the absolute and relative sizes of the program in different labor markets to the level of program success in those labor markets. There will be a wide range of program sizes which may be used to predict the effects of program growth or cutbacks. For example, if the program has higher average benefits in areas where only five percent of the poor participate as compared with areas with higher participation rates, program expansion would be expected to reduce average benefits, all other factors held constant.

As changes occur in program size this will usually mean changes in the type of program participants. It is likely that programs have differential effects depending on the type of participants. Therefore, if the evaluations can determine the average effects of the programs on different groups of participants this can be used to predict the effects of changes in program size with increased participation by particular groups.[15] Similarly, if changes in program size involve changes in program components, knowledge of the average benefits for each component will be useful. Gradually, as the number of manpower evaluations increase, more exact measures of the effects of program size will become available. Then, presumably the experience of older programs can be transferred to new ones. Meanwhile, however, we should seek to measure the impact of programs on subgroups of the participants, for components of the program, and in different areas.

Time Period Covered by the Evaluation

Measurements of program impact, as distinguished from indicators of success discussed in the next chapter, should occur no

---

[15] The average benefits of a group may not equal the benefits for the last member of that group who participates in the program. If, however, the effects of the programs on the groups under consideration differ greatly, the use of average benefits for subgroups will probably approximate more closely the marginal effects of the change in program size than will the average return for all program participants.

sooner than one year after the end of the program for the sample of participants. To examine any shorter period would raise problems of seasonality and put too great an emphasis on factors connected with the program which have only short run effects. Evaluations should also be made at three or five year intervals after the program participants have terminated.

Variables such as earnings and employment should be measured for the entire post-program period as well as for the individual years. Such measurements will demonstrate the total effect of the program and changes in program effects over time.

In these evaluations, too, the period of review should cover full years in order to avoid seasonal variations. Care should also be taken to ensure that the data are collected for identical time periods for both the experimental and control groups. Otherwise, problems with cyclical fluctuations may arise.

Sources of Data on Program Impact. Direct contact has been the basic method used to collect information about the program participants and control group members. Special studies usually used personal interviews, while the government follow-up system relied primarily on mail questionnaires and telephone interviews. The problems with direct contact are well known: there may be response error, the response rates on personal interviews seldom are above 80 percent and those on mail questionnaires are considerably lower, and direct contact is time consuming and costly. Yet for many variables which are affected by manpower programs this is the only source of information.

The random selection technique which we presented earlier should reduce some of the problems associated with contacting the individuals. Since it is known for which individuals data will subsequently be collected, special efforts can be made to remain in contact with them during and after the program. For instance, sample members may be given stamped cards to report all changes of address, the names of relatives and others who would know the location of the respondent could be secured, and the need for follow-up information could be impressed on the sample members. This should aid in achieving a higher response rate and reducing the costs of the survey, particularly when contact needs to be maintained only for one year after the program.

Because of the variety of information on dependent variables needed at the end of the first year following the program, personal contact appears to be the best for the first evaluation of manpower programs. Subsequent evaluations may consider the use of existing records.

Social Security Administration Data. For earnings data direct contact may not be necessary. The Social Security Administration will have earnings information by quarter for all covered employment.

Several problems are involved in the use of these data. First, coverage under the Social Security Act has not been universal. Of particular importance to the persons likely to participate in the manpower programs are the exclusion of federal employees, employees of government and nonprofit organizations whose employers did not volunteer for coverage, and railroad employees. In addition wages paid to domestics and on "odd jobs" often may not have been reported either because the worker did not earn the $50 per quarter minimum from the employer or because both the employer and employee were ignorant of the law. Coverage excludes approximately 10 percent of all employment.

Next, for the years 1959 to 1966, only the first $4800 of covered earnings were taxable. In 1966 the taxable limit was raised to $6600, and in 1968 it became $7800. Employers were required to report only these amounts. Consequently, individuals who have reported earnings equal to the taxable limits, in fact, had greater earnings. Therefore, the reported earnings have to be extrapolated. Some individuals, however, have reported earnings in excess of the limits. In a few cases these higher reported earnings could have been caused by "overreporting" of employers. While employers are required to report earnings only up to the taxable limits, some choose to report earnings beyond those required. In this case the relationship of the recorded actual earnings would depend on how much the employer chose to report. More often, however, recorded earnings above the maximum are due to employment in more than one job covered by social security during the year. In this situation, the individual may not have earned the taxable limit on either of the jobs, or he might have reached the taxable limit on one or more of the jobs. To determine which was the case requires visual checks of individual records which increases the cost and time involved. The general policy of the Social Security Administration is to make data resources available, but within recognizable limits. Such limits include safeguarding the confidentiality of information on individuals so that data will not be provided on specific individuals. Data will be provided, however, in tabular form including the sum of squares and cross products for the entire sample or subgroups of the sample (containing more than four persons) as designated by the researcher.

Finally, there is a time lag between the end of the calendar year and when the data are posted. Approximately 98 percent of nonfarm and 90 percent of farm wages are posted by the end of the following October. But only 65 percent of self-employment records are posted then and it takes another six months before 90 percent are posted. Thus complete data are not available until nearly one and a half years after the end of the year being examined. In addition, further time may be required by the Social Security Administration before they can handle the job.

For long term follow-ups of individuals, however, this may be the only source of information available. It may not be possible to locate many individuals after many years have elapsed. The mobility of individuals in manpower programs is high. The Social Security Administration, on the other hand, will always have complete and relatively accurate data.

Tax Data. The Internal Revenue Service (IRS) will provide earnings data as contained on the 1040 series. If coded variables of the individual's background characteristics, along with their social security numbers, are sent to the IRS, they will provide tabular summaries on individual income data, provided three or more individuals share the same coded characteristics and that the identifying social security numbers are omitted. Data are usually available for a year by the late summer of the following year.

The main obstacle for effective utilization of this procedure is the lack of identification as to the source of earnings, an important consideration for married persons who file a joint return. Combined earnings of husband and wife cannot be properly identified. Thus these data are of greatest use for evaluating youth programs where most participants will file single returns.

Arrangements for this service are made through the Assistant Commissioner for Research and Planning of the IRS. Since access to the main files are limited, priorities are established by the IRS.

Unemployment Insurance Wage Data. Thirty-seven states and the District of Columbia require all employers covered by their unemployment insurance laws to report the quarterly earnings of all covered employees. All earnings are reported; there is no limit to the amount. Also, posting of these data is usually complete within three months of the end of a quarter. Thus employment compensation data do not suffer from two of the major faults of social security data.

There are other problems. The thirteen states which do not collect this data include many of the major industrial states. Even in the states which do collect the data, coverage is not extended to the self-employed, domestics, farm workers, or persons who work for immediate relatives. Also not covered are employees of small firms (the minimum size varies from state to state) or employees of nonprofit or governmental units. Nationally, only about 65 percent of the labor force are in covered employment. Finally, there is no way to identify an individual who has left the state rather than become unemployed or left the labor force. In all three cases there would be no record of earnings.

Thus the unemployment insurance data will be most useful for short-term follow-ups in industrial areas. In these cases it will provide accurate data quickly for most of the sample. For longer periods when the person is more likely to have left the state, the social security data, which is national, appear to be a better alternative.

Projecting the Benefits. Manpower programs may affect the participants for the remainder of their lives. Obviously, the decisionmaker cannot wait that long before he must judge the program. Therefore, a one year follow-up with subsequent evaluations was proposed. The early evaluations will require, however, that observed benefits be projected into the future in order to estimate the total gains from the program. Several methods might be used to make these projections.

The most logical method would be to base the projection on the experience of participants in other programs. If the gains from a similar program have increased at an annual rate of 5 percent, then this same figure could be applied. Unfortunately, we have not built up a basis for comparison. Most manpower programs and all of the evaluations of them are less than ten years old. Longitudinal data is not yet available on them.[16] Therefore, while definite

---

[16] Two studies which deal with the longer term effects of retraining are Gerald G. Somers and Graeme H. McKechnie, "Vocational Retraining Programs for the Unemployed," and Michael E. Borus, "Time Trends in the Benefits from Retraining." Both appeared in the *1967 Proceedings of the Industrial Relations Research Association,* Madison: Industrial Relations Research Association, 1968.

efforts should be made to secure these data, at present some other less satisfactory method will have to be used.

The best method appears to be the projection of benefits for several periods with benefits increasing, remaining constant, and declining. The longer term projections should take mortality and labor force participation rates into account. A matrix can be constructed which presents the expected benefits under each of the alternatives (e.g. Table 1). Such a matrix will show the sensitivity of the benefits to various combinations of assumptions, which should be useful when comparing different programs.

Table 1. Total Benefits under Alternative Assumptions

Period of Benefit Life	Benefits Decline by an Amount Which Will Cause Them to Be Zero at the End of the Period	Benefits Are Constant	Benefits Increase at 5 Percent per Year
5 Years			
10 Years			
20 Years			
Until Participant Reaches 65			

As longitudinal studies provide more hard data on the time trends in benefits the matrix can be condensed. Until then considerable thought should be given to determining which description of the particular benefit studied is most appropriate. For example, nearly all manpower programs attempt to place an individual on a higher career ladder than he would otherwise attain. To the extent that he is put into entry level jobs on a new ladder instead of remaining stationary on his former rungs, the benefits may grow over time. On the other hand, the jobs which are presently vacant would not continue to remain vacant indefinitely: from society's point of view the benefits may decline over time. Merely filling in the matrix is only the first step in projecting benefits. Theoretical considerations must follow.

Assigning Value to Future Benefits—The Use of Discount Rates. Few individuals would be indifferent about receiving the same

amount of income now or in the future.[17] These preferences for
the present over the future must be taken into account in evaluations
of manpower programs for such programs involve giving up of
present resources in order to have greater future resources. Since
the stream of benefits will vary for different programs, a comparison
of these programs will require both streams to be valued at the
same point in time. The usual procedure is to calculate the value
of a program's benefits as of the conclusion of the program.

The cost of manpower programs to society, the government,
and the individual are all immediate while the benefits accrue
over many years. Making the two equivalent requires the benefits
to be reduced so that they may be found at the time when costs
are incurred.

There is no single rate of discount which is appropriate for use
in all cases. The discount rate should be no lower than the return
the funds could earn in alternative investments nor should it be
lower than the amount people are willing to pay to borrow funds
to increase consumption. These rates differ, however, based on
who is investing and borrowing. The government borrowing rate,
which is practically risk free to the lender, is approximately 4 to 6
percent. Business faces a somewhat higher rate and the individual
faces many borrowing rates ranging from 6 percent to over 25
percent depending on the risk involved to the lender.

The alternative investment opportunities also vary. The basic
alternative to a government program is a tax cut which will allow
private business investment. The return on private investment is
in the range of 10 to 20 percent, part of which is a premium for
risk. The return to the individual typically is lower, 5 to 15 percent,
again depending on the risk involved. Since the extent of risk
is not known in the investment cases, the true rate of return is not
known for alternative projects. To quote A. R. Prest and R. Turvey,
two economists chosen by the American Economic Association and
the Royal Economic Society to survey the field of cost-benefit
analysis, "the truth of the matter is that, whatever one does, one

---

[17] The proverb "A bird in the hand is worth two in the bush" applies to
the benefits of manpower programs, and in particular the monetary benefits.
A dollar received now can be spent for current consumption (the bird in the
hand) or can be invested to produce greater future consumption (to get the
two birds from the bush).

is trying to unscramble an omelette, and no one has yet invented a uniquely superior way of doing this."[18]

Therefore, the most logical way to proceed is to consider a variety of possible discount rates and then test how sensitive the analysis is to each choice. Rates of 5 percent, 10 percent and 15 percent would appear to be the best rates to use. For most manpower program comparisons the relative values of the benefits of two programs will vary little with the discount rate which is selected. The use of a discount rate is necessary, however, if programs having different time streams of benefits are to be compared.[19]

---

[18] A. R. Prest and Ralph Turvey, "Cost-Benefit Analysis: A Survey," *Surveys of Economic Theory: Resource Allocations,* New York: St. Martin's Press, 1966, p. 172.

[19] For further discussion of discount rates see U. S. Congress, Joint Economic Committee, *The Analysis and Evaluation of Public Expenditures: The PPBS System.* A compendium of papers submitted to the Subcommittee on Economy in Government, 3 volumes. Washington: U. S. Government Printing Office, 1969.

4

THE DEVELOPMENT OF SHORT-TERM INDICATORS OF SUCCESS

A basic dilemma appears to exist in evaluating the impact of manpower programs. Operating agencies need data on the success of the program as the participants go through the program and at their termination from it. This information must be available in order to modify the program to achieve maximum operating efficiency. Likewise, decisionmakers need immediate evaluations of individual projects in order to eliminate the bad ones and to extend the best practices of the good ones.[1] Studies of program impact, however, do not typically provide these data because such studies usually are interested only in the long run consequences of the programs.

The impact evaluations should make a useful contribution to operating decision, though. They should develop indicators, that can be measured during and at the end of the program, which

---

[1] For a discussion of other uses of short-term indicators see Worth Bateman, "Assessing Program Effectiveness," *Welfare in Review,* January-February 1968, pp. 1-10.

will predict the long run success of program participants. Those which predict success accurately could then be used by the operating agencies to improve this and future programs, and reduce the necessity for future major studies of impact. For example, if good attendance during the program correlates highly with measures of long run success for certain MDTA retraining classes, the operating agencies can then use this as an indication of the success of future retraining classes and similar manpower programs, such as the Work Incentive Program.

Procedures for Selecting Indicators of Success

The urgent need for short-term measures of program success has been recognized by the agencies charged with evaluating manpower programs. Numerous criteria have been applied (and thus implicitly used as predictors of long run success). Yet, the predictive abilities of few, if any, have been tested. We, therefore, need to validate the measures presently being used and to explore the predictive powers of others. In making these explorations we should recognize that many of the possible indicators will not be good predictors.

To determine the relative values of the short-term indicators would require measurement of each of the potential indicators at the time of the program.[2] These data would be saved until the long run success of the programs had been calculated. Then all of the indicators would be correlated with each of the measures of long run success. Wherever a high positive or negative correlation existed this would indicate that a good indicator had been found. Those which accurately predicted the success or failure of various groups then could be used by the operating agencies as criteria to judge the value of their procedures and programs. Thus, in this way, the impact evaluation would concern itself not only with the long run effects but also with improving the short run efficiency of manpower programs.

The earlier in the project accurate indicators can be found, the more useful the indicators become for modifying the program.

---

[2] The random selection technique again would be most useful here since the variables which would be examined could be detailed prior to the program. Retrospective studies, on the other hand, would probably be unable to find indicators of success, since they would have to rely solely on whatever data happened to have been collected for the project.

Primary attention should be focused on finding indicators during the time the participants are in the projects. To the extent that these are not available, indicators at the conclusion of the program and in the immediate post-program period should be sought. Using time of recording as a criterion, possible indicators of future success can be divided into four categories: program operating efficiency, participant attitudes, program short-term goal achievement, and immediate post-program success.

Program Operating Efficiency

The first set of indicators will vary somewhat with the program being evaluated. Each program is designed to perform a number of functions for the participants in that program. Since it is assumed that each function will improve some aspect of the participants' employability, it is useful to determine how well these functions are being performed. Direct observation of project operations will usually be the means for assessment. Some of the measures of efficiency will be:

1. The quality of the program staff. Staff can be evaluated in terms of their backgrounds and training relative to the services they perform, their competency in performing these services, their commitment to the project, their ability to supervise and interact with the program participants, their morale and extent of turnover, their integrity, and their flexibility and innovativeness in dealing with new situations. While subjective ratings cannot be avoided, it would be desirable to develop rating criteria and scales to measure each of these items.

2. The use of suitable facilities for carrying out the objectives of the program. For example, the facilities should be near to the target population, they should have the equipment necessary to perform any training and they should have enough space to carry on counseling, job development, and similar activities.

3. The actual establishment of all the components and services considered necessary for the program. For newer programs, the establishment of these services within specified time periods will also be necessary.

4. The development and maintenance of records suitable: (a) to measure participants' activities and flow through the program components, (b) to identify participants' aptitudes and abilities

in order to facilitate job placement after training, and (c) to provide a full accounting of program costs and payments to staff and trainees.

5. The adequacy of allowances. The participants should receive the funds necessary to permit them to live while in the program and to purchase equipment necessary to hold employment after training.

6. The positive relationships established among project staff, employers, and other community leaders. For instance, project staff should be able to refer participants effectively to other organizations in order to receive needed services. Similarly, employers should be made to view the project as a source of present or future recruitment.

7. The evenness of the flow of participants through the program and the time spent at each stage. There should be paths which connect the series of services provided to each individual. Presumably, an efficient program will have a relatively even flow along these paths. Individuals should not be placed in a "holding status" once they have begun the program.

8. The adequacy of each service performed relative to the needs of the participants and the amount of the service proposed in the program design. Care should be taken to ensure that individuals are not provided with a service unnecessarily, as well as provided too little of a service.

9. The type of enrollee to whom the program provides services. If the program is aimed at particular segments of the population, the percentage of the target groups who are enrolled in the program and the percentage of enrollees who are from the target group should probably be high if the program is to be successful.[3]

Participants' Attitudes

Another set of indicators of program success are evaluations of the program made by the participants. Participants' attitudes toward, and their evaluations of, the personnel, the instruction, if any, the procedures followed by the project, the objectives of the project, and the success of the project may be useful predictors

---

[3] It is recognized that secondary effects may affect a target group even though it does not participate in the program. Until techniques are developed to identify these secondary effects, one must assume that programs will not affect the earnings and employment of target groups if they do not participate in the program.

of project success. In addition, the criticism which may be elicited may be used to improve the project.

In addition to the oral or written expression of attitudes much can be gathered from the behavior of the participants. Absences or tardiness without adequate reasons, and nonattentive, antisocial or interruptive behavior during the project may be correlated with lack of success. Likewise, completion of the program may be an important determinant of success. Therefore, information should be collected on the proportion of participants who do not complete the program and on many of their characteristics. These persons also should be asked: (1) their reasons for dropping out; (2) the amount of knowledge they gained in the program which they subsequently used; (3) the characteristics of the jobs they took after dropping out, (including their rate of pay, their average number of hours of work, the occupation and industry in which they work, and the relationship of the program to their job), and their future job prospects.

Program Short-Run Goal Achievement

As discussed above each of the services performed for the participants has a short-run goal which is designed to ultimately improve the individual's employability. For example, skill training such as provided by MDTA seeks to make the participants more employable or to raise their incomes by improving their abilities to perform on a job; work-experience programs seek to improve the work habits and attitudes of the individuals and thus make them more acceptable for employment; and child care services are designed to increase participation in the labor force. Both during the program and at its completion, the degree of success in attaining each of these short-run goals can be measured. This is seen by examining the measures of short-run success for a list of program functions.[4] These measures may be examined equally well relative to the needs of the program as it exists, relative to the program as planned to arrive at design efficiency, or relative to expenditures to measure cost efficiency. The first of these is presented here.

---

[4] It is doubtful that many of these short-run criteria will be accurate predictors of long run program success. We are presenting all of them here, because at this time studies have not been conducted to eliminate those which are not predictors.

Table 2. Possible Short-Run Goals and Criteria

Short-Run Goals	*Criteria of Short-Run Goal Achievement*
1. Locate individuals who could benefit from manpower programs	Number of persons identified as a proportion of the "universe of need"
2. Recruit people into the labor force	Number of persons entering programs who would not otherwise be in the labor force as a proportion of program openings
3. Interest workers in manpower programs	Number of applicants and enrollees as a proportion of program openings
4. Determine persons' interests toward work	Number of preemployment interviews conducted as a proportion of participants
5. Determine worker aptitudes and abilities	Number of persons counseled and tested with GATB and other instruments as a proportion of participants
6. Determine mental and physical health needs and provide necessary services	Number of physical, eye, and dental examinations and amount and nature of services performed relative to the needs of the participants
7. Determine existence and nature of personal or family problems	Number of personal counseling sessions and nature of problems identified as a percentage of participants
8. Improve attitudes toward work	Improvement in scores on attitude scales
9. Improve worker appearance and social acceptability	Improvement in score on a rating scale measuring these items
10. Increase educational levels	Improvement in score on Metropolitan, Stanford or Wide Range achievement tests
11. Increase skill levels	Improvement in score on work sampling tests
12. Solve personal or family problems	Number of therapy or counseling sessions and nature of problems solved
13. Provide legal services	Amount and nature of services provided relative to needs of participants
14. Provide funds for subsistence	Amount of funds provided relative to estimated needs of family

Table 2. Possible Short-Run Goals and Criteria (Cont.)

Short-Run Goals	Criteria of Short-Run Goal Achievement
15. Provide loans to improve employability	Amount of funds and uses of those funds relative to needs
16. Improve knowledge of the labor market	Improvement in participants' knowledge of job openings, wage rates, and unemployment in the labor area
17. Restructure jobs and change job requirements	Number of jobs restructured and nature of changes made relative to qualifications of the unemployed
18. Change hiring requirements	Number and nature of changes and increase in hiring as a proportion of unemployed
19. Find job openings	Number of openings found and new job orders placed relative to existing occupational needs of the unemployed
20. Educate employers to needs of workers	Improvement in employer attitudes as measured by interview data and attitude scales
21. Refer and place in jobs	Number of referrals and placements made as a proportion of unemployed. The reduction in the time necessary to make placements. The relation of the job requirements of the referrals and placements, to the individual aptitudes and abilities of the unemployed
22. Provide transportation to employment	Number of persons transported who would not otherwise be able to get to work as a percentage of the unemployed
23. Eliminate labor shortages	Percentage reduction in the average number of vacancies in particular occupations where labor shortages limit the number of hires, and the length of time vacancies exist. Vacancy measures may be based on job orders with the ES or vacancies listed in a job vacancy survey.
24. Provide day care	Number of persons able to work because of care for dependents as a proportion of unemployed.

Table 2. Possible Short-Run Goals and Criteria (Cont.)

Short-Run Goals	Criteria of Short-Run Goal Achievement
25. Solve on-the-job problems of workers	Number of counseling sessions conducted and types of problems solved as a proportion of counseling needs
26. Solve problems of employer dealing with worker once he is on the job	Improvement in the scores of workers on job satisfaction scales
27. Subsidize geographic movement of workers to find jobs	Number of persons moved and employed as a percentage of area unemployed who are willing to move
28. Provide jobs	Number of persons employed and type of work experience provided as a proportion of the unemployed

Immediate Post-Program Success

Many of the long run measures of manpower program success may also be applied shortly after the end of the project, for example 30 days from the project's conclusion. For others, proxies may be used. Each of these immediate post-program measures of success would be based on the expected experience in the absence of the program as seen primarily from the individuals' labor market histories before the program. Some of the variables which might be measured are listed in Table 3. Again we realize that many of these variables will not predict long-run program success. We list them to suggest the possibilities which need to be tested.

Table 3. Possible Immediate Post-Program Goals and Criteria

Possible Immediate Post-Program Goals	Criteria of Immediate Post-Program Success, for all program participants and for different types of program participants
1. Reduced unemployment and increased employment	The increased percent of participants who are employed and the reduced percent unemployed, 30 days after the end of the program
2. Increased productivity of the labor force and increased earnings	The increase in average hourly earnings including the value of fringe benefits of participants. This may be measured by a comparison of pre- and post-program earnings

Table 3. Possible Immediate Post-Program Goals and Criteria (Cont.)

Possible Immediate Post-Program Goals	*Criteria of Immediate Post-Program Success, for all program participants and for different types of program participants*
2. (cont.)	with some discounting for changes in average wages in the economy over the period
3. Improved equity in the distribution of income and employment	The proportion of participants in the programs who come from various target groups and the average changes in their incomes and employment relative to the averages for society
4. Increased labor force participation rates	The increase in the percent of program participants and other family members in the labor force after the program, as compared with before it
5. Increased social satisfaction	The average improvement in scores on a test of attitudes toward social institutions, on job satisfaction tests and on scales of social indicators
6. Increased work week for those desiring more work	The increase in the average number of hours actually worked as a proportion of the number of hours of employment desired at the going wage rate
7. Placements in jobs which make full use of applicants' abilities and aptitudes	A comparison of ability and achievement test scores with job requirements of post-program placement. A rough measure might be a comparison of work sampling and GATB test scores with the D.O.T. classification for the job
8. Increased mobility of the labor force to improve their economic status	The proportion of program participants who move to secure jobs
9. Reduced unnecessary turnover	The average number of jobs from which program participants have been fired or have quit without adequate reason and without alternative employment

Table 3. Possible Immediate Post-Program Goals and Criteria (Cont.)

Possible Immediate Post-Program Goals	*Criteria of Immediate Post-Program Success,* for all program participants and for different types of program participants:
10. Reduced dependency on government	The proportion of program participants who receive welfare and unemployment compensation, and the amount received of each after the program as compared with preprogram experience. The degree of dependency as perceived by the program participants should also be examined.
11. Reduced asocial behavior	The proportions of the program participants arrested and convicted of crimes or of participating in riots
12. Improved health	The average change in the nutritional level of the program participants as measured by changes in the amount spent on food and the protein content of their diet
13. Improved housing	The change in the quality of the housing of program participants based on the Census definitions
14. Increased number of persons available for military service	The proportion of program participants reclassified as acceptable for military service
15. Jobs filled with specific employers	The proportion of participants accepting jobs in occupations where workers are in short supply. The reduction in the number and the length of vacancies and ES job orders from the labor shortage occupations is a second measure.
16. Jobs filled in particular geographic areas	The number and proportion of program participants who are placed in jobs in each city, SMSA, Congressional District, State, and region. The reduction in the number and the length of vacancies and ES job orders in each of these areas

5

THE COSTS OF
MANPOWER PROGRAMS

The costs of a manpower program most properly should be considered to be the program's opportunity cost—the value of the alternative benefits which are foregone because of the program. Resources which are devoted to the manpower program cannot be used to produce other goods and services. For instance, society by devoting manpower to conduct training programs loses the services of those persons as teachers in vocational high schools, as stock brokers, or even as automobile workers, to use a few examples. Another alternative is that these persons would be unemployed, in which case, society gives up nothing in lost production by putting them to work. Similarly, the government gives up alternative programs or tax cuts and employers give up plant improvements or dividends when they spend funds for manpower programs. Finally, individuals may lose earnings while they participate in the program.

It is often difficult, however, to identify opportunity costs. We consequently often must limit ourselves to measuring the value of the resources used on the assumption that the factors of production receive an amount approximating the value of their production in other uses. This assumption of no economic rents assumes profit maximization, perfect competition in all markets, that the programs are only operating at the margin and that there are no externalities, to be perfectly correct. Given the relatively small scale of manpower programs, however, the nonexistence of all of the assumed conditions may not be particularly important, especially for cross-program comparisons.

The costs of manpower programs can be viewed from several different perspectives, just as were their benefits. As explained above, society, individual program participants, employers, and government may each be required to give up resources for use in the programs. In some cases expenditures of resources will mean foregone opportunities for more than one group. For example, salaries of government administrators will be costs for society as well as for the government. There will also be expenditures, however, which will be costs for one group but will be gains for other groups, for example government allowance payments to program participants or reimbursements paid to employers will be costs for the government but will actually reduce the costs of the participants and the firms involved.[1] Therefore, we once again present separate lists for each group.

I. Costs For Society

A.   The time spent by all personnel involved in the program. Special care should be taken to include the time of the following groups who are often not considered.

  1.   The local project staff, who are not engaged full-time in the program. The costs should include the value of the time they spend on such activities as: design of the project proposal; recruitment, testing, and counseling of prospective participants; the provision of any supportive services connected with the program such as legal services, counseling, custodial care of the equipment and facilities used by the program, day care services, health services,

---

[1] As a general rule, all changes in resources and funds which occur during the program are considered as costs and all changes after the program are considered as benefits. There may be gains during the program such as higher income for the participants but it is easier to treat these as negative costs.

remedial education, and transportation; processing allow-ance payments; job development; skill training; job referral and placement; follow-up counseling; evaluative follow-up; and all of the record keeping and other administrative tasks involved in each of the programs.

2. The persons at the regional and state levels who are in any way involved in the program. Included would be consultants to local projects, field supervisors, persons responsible for project approval and review, and statisticians involved in reviewing project reports. Again, their salaries should be allocated in proportion to the time spent on the program.

3. The personnel in the national offices of the U. S. Department of Labor and other agencies involved in manpower programs. Their salaries should be allocated in proportion to the time spent on administration of the program including budgetary review, fiscal accounting, policy planning, project approval, project monitoring and evaluation, research, and training of staff.

B. The physical capital used in the program. This would include:
   1. The market rental value of all property and buildings including government property
   2. The market rental value of all machines, instructional equipment and supplies, and other materials used in the program. Equipment which is purchased should be depreciated based on use. Where it is not possible to estimate depreciation on a use basis, the difference between original cost and salvage value should be amortized appropriately over the life of the program.

C. Miscellaneous services which are necessary to the operation of the program, such as staff travel, telephone services and equipment repairs

D. The goods and services purchased by the program participants which they would not otherwise have had to buy. These include such expenditures as: transportation to and from the program, meals and living expenses away from home, uniforms, books, tools or other educational materials and day care for dependents.

E. The potential production of persons participating in the program which is lost during the time the program is being conducted. Included would be the output of the program participants which would occur in the absence of the program.

II. Participant Costs of Manpower Programs

A. The expenditure which the program participants make for items they would not need if they did not participate in the program. These items are discussed in section I-D.

B. The after tax earnings lost because of participation in the program minus any increased government payments received as an inducement to enter the program. The latter would include training allowances, subsistence allowances, travel allowances, trainee wages, and higher welfare payments or unemployment insurance payments than would otherwise be received.

III. Employer Costs of Manpower Programs

A. The wage costs of employees who perform services similar to those presented in section I-A, minus any funds received from the government to reimburse the firm

B. The value of all physical capital used up in the program which is owned by the firm and for which it does not receive reimbursement from the government. These items are the same as those discussed in section I-B.

C. Miscellaneous expenditures by the firm on services necessary for program operations which are not reimbursed by the government. These may be the items included in section I-C.

D. The production lost because of poor quality of work which results as a part of the learning process for the participants. From this cost any reductions in taxes as a result of lower profits and any reimbursement from the government should be subtracted.

IV. Government Costs of Manpower Programs

A. The personnel costs of all personnel involved in the program for whom the government pays the salaries or reimburses local sponsors. Personnel to be considered include those discussed in section I-A.

B. The value of all physical capital used in the program which is government owned, rented by government, or for which a local sponsor is reimbursed. The items for consideration are those presented in section I-B.

C. The expenditures on miscellaneous services which are made by government or for which payment is reimbursed by government.

D. The net increase in government payments to individuals which are made to induce them to participate in the programs. These would include the items discussed in section II-B.

E. The tax revenues which are lost during the program. These would include the reductions in the personal income taxes, social security taxes and unemployment insurance taxes which may result from lower earnings, and the reductions in sales and excise taxes caused by lower expenditures of the participants while they are in the program. In addition, lower corporate profits taxes might result from decreased efficiency of participants involved in on-the-job programs.

F. The other items for which government makes payments to local sponsors. These would include payments to firms conducting on-the-job training to compensate for the lower productivity of trainees.

6

MEASURING THE COSTS OF MANPOWER PROGRAMS

Just as the proper measurement of program success was based on the comparison of outcomes with and without the program, this is also the key to proper measurement of program costs. Only those costs should be considered which involve the loss of some benefit which would have accrued in the absence of the program. Since, as discussed above, opportunity costs are difficult to measure, calculation of costs must often consider instead the value of the resources devoted to the program. In this circumstance only the increment in resource use should be measured. For example, most manpower programs involve a job referral component. When calculating the cost of this component, the expenditures by the employment service which would have been made for job referral for these individuals even had the program not existed must be subtracted from the program expenditure on this item. Only if this is done will the increment in the resources used by manpower programs be calculated, and it is only this concept which can be compared with the measures of additional well-being which were discussed earlier.

Measuring Incremental Resource Use

To measure the costs of a program requires the comparison of the opportunity cost or the expenditure of resources on behalf of the program participants by themselves, by society, by government or by employers, with those which would have occurred were there no program. We should note again that while we desire to measure the effects of adding or subtracting participants from the program, we usually are unable to do this. Instead we measure the average costs for a program and must assume that the program with higher average costs will have a higher cost for adding a new participant.

As was the case with measurements of program success, the best way to measure what would have happened to the program participants is to use a control group which is randomly selected from persons willing and able to enter the program. Again, only this group will give an unbiased estimate. Thus if costs are to be accurately estimated, the same type of control group must be used to measure them as is used to measure program success. If projects are selected for evaluation when funded, this will permit the same control groups to be used to measure the costs and success of a program.

The Use of Control Groups. Control groups should be used to provide information for three types of cost estimates. The first is the losses incurred while the participants are in the manpower program (the opportunity costs). While participating in the program, individuals usually are not engaged in what they normally would be doing. Therefore, participation in the program may lead to losses of after tax earnings, unemployment compensation, or welfare payments by the individuals; production by society; and taxes by government. The experience of the control group during the course, however, should not be affected by the program. This assumes that the program is not so large as to affect the entire labor market. Therefore, the difference between their after tax earnings, unemployment compensation, welfare payments, production, and taxes, and those of the program participants will show the losses actually incurred because of participation in the program.

The second use of control groups is to determine how much of the governmental services received by the participants would not have been received if there were no program. Earlier we discussed employment service job referral services which are normally used by many of the persons who enter manpower programs. Similarly when welfare recipients enter manpower programs the counseling they receive in the program may merely replace counseling they would have received from a case worker. Therefore it is important that information be collected on the amount and nature of all governmental services received by both the participants and the control group. If this is known, the latter can be subtracted from the former to find the actual increment in services which result from a program. Then only the cost of this increment in services should be compared with the benefits which were calculated as the differences between the two groups.

Finally, the control group can be used to measure the increment in program related expenditures by the participants. Some programs require the participants to incur expenses for travel, instructional materials, uniforms, living expenses and meals away from home, etc. Some of these expenditures represent added costs of program participation. Others, however, may not. For example, if an individual would be taking the bus to work instead of taking it to a training center were he not in a manpower program, there may be no additional cost of transportation resulting from the program. To arrive at this conclusion, however, it is necessary to know the expenditures associated with the course by the participants and the expenditures on these items by the control group. Therefore information of this sort should be obtained.

Measuring Costs for Other Family Members. In addition to the control groups, measurements should also be made for other persons who might be affected by the program. One group which is very likely to be affected are the participants' families. For instance, if participation lowers the earnings of the participant, the slack may be taken up by another family member who accepts a temporary job which he would not normally have taken. Such changes could be discovered by comparing the work experiences during the program, not only of the participants and members of the control groups but also their respective families.

Measuring the Costs for Other Groups. Manpower programs may also affect the circumstances of groups entirely unrelated to program participants. This would be particularly true if the participants forego jobs while they are in the programs. Under these circumstances there may be a number of secondary persons who would otherwise be unemployed or employed at lower paying positions, who are able to fill these jobs. Society in these cases loses the output of the program participant but gains the output of the secondary groups. Overall there may be no net loss to society. Similarly the government will not necessarily lose tax revenues or pay increased transfer payments. When the secondary individuals find employment, the government welfare and unemployment payments to them may fall. These could offset the government losses on the participants.

Alternatively, if the program involves work experience or on-the-job training, the program participant may be displacing someone else who would have been doing this work. If this second person is unemployed (or causes someone else to become unemployed) the output of the program participants should not be included in its entirety as a negative cost in calculating the costs of the program to society. Similarly, calculations of government costs should take the displacement effect into consideration by estimating the tax reductions and the increase in transfer payments which result for the second party.

Because these effects on second parties may either decrease or increase the costs of manpower programs substantially, the secondary effects must be measured to get an accurate accounting. Unfortunately, no methodology for measurement has as yet been developed. This should be one of the first steps in future manpower program evaluation research.

The Use of Multivariate Analysis

In our discussion of the measurement of program success we indicated that multivariate analysis should be used to determine how the personal characteristics, the program characteristics, and exogeneous factors affected each of the goals. The same procedures should be used to examine costs. Only if this is done will it be possible to relate differing program success which results from changing the nature of the program with the costs for making these changes. For example, if the job development component is found to be twice as effective as the counseling component, one must also know the relative costs of the two sets of components before any changes are introduced. Thus the costs for society, participants, employers, and government should each be analyzed using the same independent variables as we discussed in the section on benefits.

The multivariate analysis of costs, however, can be conducted on two levels. The first is to examine total costs of projects. Each project examined in the study is an observation and total project cost, total project cost per enrollee, total project cost per graduate, or total project cost per hour of enrollee participation can be the dependent variables. Such an analysis could tell the effect on total costs of changing the characteristics mix of the participants or of changing the components which make up the program. This is the type of average cost information which is usually desired. If, however, it was useful to know the effect of such changes on the costs of particular components of the program then the dependent variable would have to be only the cost of that component, the cost of the component per enrollee or graduate or the cost of the component per hour of participation.

Another approach would be to treat each participant in the program as the unit of observation. This type of analysis is analogous to that used to measure program success and could also provide more detailed information because there would be a greater number of observations. It is, however, much more difficult to conduct. Data are not now kept on an individual basis.

The data required, though, would be the same as those which we felt necessary to estimate the effect of changes in program components. Each individual participant would need a form on which would be entered all services performed in the program for the individual, the time spent in providing these services and the identity of the person who provides them. The costs of the services would then be computed by multiplying the hourly rate of each person providing services by the amount of time provided. To this would be added a figure representing some apportionment of the administrative costs, the costs of capital facilities, and the cost of miscellaneous services. The apportionment might be based on the length of time the participant was in the program. Finally, the individual's additional expenditures and opportunity costs of being in the program would be added. These individual costs would be the dependent variable with the same independent variables as discussed earlier.

Accurately Measuring the Costs

Our discussion of the measurement of costs to this point has been abbreviated. The reasons should be obvious. The type of analysis and the independent variables are identical to those used for measuring program success. The use of control groups is also similar. There is, however, a major problem in measuring costs which does not exist in the measurement of program benefits.

The government accounting systems are designed on an appropriations basis and not on the basis of incremental costs. As a result, many items are improperly charged to a program while other costs are ignored. Thus to accurately calculate the costs of manpower programs, it is necessary to include the expenditures actually made as a part of the program. The outline in the preceding chapter presents several areas which are normally not included in the calculation of manpower programs. Additional problem areas follow.

Proper Program Assignment. The costs of functions performed for a program sometimes are not charged to that program. For example, in the Neighborhood Youth Corps (NYC) program one sponsor may devote staff time to recruitment, and to sponsor may use employment service (ES) staff to carry out these functions. Under present accounting these costs are all assigned to the NYC in the former case and all assigned to the ES in the latter case. Yet the same services are being performed for the NYC participants in the two areas. Therefore, in many situations one must go beyond the costs directly assigned to a program in order to include all of them. Other examples of often improperly assigned costs are: remedial education in the NYC program which is sometimes provided by the local school systems, the use of school buildings and equipment for training programs, the time spent by various public officials preparing project proposals, and the value of the services of persons on loan from business.

Similarly, if expenditures are assigned to a program but in fact are made in part for other programs, only a portion of their costs should be included. For instance, equipment purchased for one program subsequently may be used for others (such as machines brought for a training class which are subsequently used in other classes or for vocational education purposes, or persons who are hired for one project may devote part of their time to designing proposals for other projects).

Inclusion of All Costs. All of the costs of a program should be measured. Yet, there are several items which typically have not been included. The first of these was discussed above, the value of public facilities provided free of charge. While the use of these facilities does not represent an outlay of funds, there are still costs involved.

Most equipment will wear out with use. Consequently, use by the manpower programs will accelerate the need for replacement or repair. Therefore, the depreciation of these types of equipment should be calculated and included in the costs of the programs. This will be particularly important for the instructional equipment used in manpower training courses.

Even for buildings, which will suffer little from the additional wear, there will still be costs associated with their use by manpower programs. Other activities may be displaced. For instance, if a vocational high school is used for training, vocational education classes may have to be held elsewhere or may not be held at all. Both of these alternatives will involve costs. Similarly, even when an abandoned army base is used as a Job Corps camp there are costs because the property could always be sold or leased to private industry. Thus to measure the true cost of these facilities, they should be valued at their market rental value.

The administrative cost of manpower programs is another category which typically is underreported. There is a large administrative overhead connected with each program. Many of these items are included in I-A-2 and I-A-3 of the outline. All of the time of the civil servants at the national and regional levels spent on planning the original program, budget and proposal approval, project review and monitoring, program connected evaluation and research, fiscal appropriations and accounting, and on all other administrative duties involved in program operation at these levels should be considered. Ideally, the time spent by each government worker, from the Secretary of Labor on down, should be apportioned between programs and if possible between particular projects.

Greater attempts should be made to approximate the costs of each of these categories since they represent sizeable costs which presently are excluded from most calculations.

Examining the Costs of the First Program Participants

The cost of a particular manpower program will vary depending on when in the course of the program's development the measurement is made. As with most businesses the costs of manpower programs will decline as their scale and life increases. A program will have relatively high costs per participant when it is being developed and the number of participants is small. Program staff will be engaged in training personnel, establishing bookkeeping systems, writing proposals, experimenting with program ideas and similar organizing functions. As the program becomes more established and experience is gained, less time will be spent on these activities and more time can be devoted to the participants, increasing the number of participants and reducing unit costs. While the benefits may not change with program size it is almost certain that the program costs will change. Therefore, the time period used to measure the costs of a program will be crucial, particularly at the beginning of a program.

To resolve the problem for a new program, we suggest that the benefits of the first program participants should be related to the administratrative costs for later participants in the program.[1] For the first group of program participants, the government and sponsor administrative cost data which are to be compared with program benefits should be the costs of the program after it has become more established. This would cause the costs assigned to the first group of program participants to be below those actually incurred. It would, however, give a better indication of the long run costs of the program. Moreover, it would not lead to any delay in the evaluation since the program success of the participants will not be measured until one year after they complete the program and the actual costs incurred could be used for subsequent groups of program participants.

---

[1] Cost data still should be gathered at the start of the program for comparisons with latter cost figures to find the extent of decline in costs with increases in the size of the program and for administrative purposes.

7

COMBINING THE MEASURES OF PROGRAM SUCCESS AND COST

The data gathered for evaluations of manpower programs should provide the information to make four types of decisions: (1) whether a particular existing program should be continued, (2) which of several alternative existing programs should be expanded or contracted, (3) in what ways can changes in the components of a particular program lead to improved efficiency, and (4) for particular groups of individuals, what programs serve them best? The data discussed in the previous chapters will provide the answers to these questions.

Making Program Decisions

In the second section of this primer we outlined a series of many different types of possible criteria for measuring program success. Any or all of these criteria may be considered to be important by a decisionmaker evaluating a program. Therefore, a measure of program success and cost should be calculated for every criterion which has been examined in the analysis.

Combinations of Program Success and Cost Measures. The basic tools for combining measures of program success and cost are as benefit-cost and cost-effectiveness ratios.[1] These express the average amount of success per dollar of cost, which should be measured in terms of present value, i.e.,

$$\frac{\text{total success}}{\text{total cost}} \quad \text{or} \quad \frac{\text{average success}}{\text{average cost}}$$

Usually, both terms in the ratio will be positive. This indicates that there is some success from the program but that this involves the use of resources to accomplish this gain. When a benefit-cost ratio is greater than one, it indicates that the present value of the economic returns exceeds the costs of the program. If the ratio is less than one, this indicates that the program costs more than the value of the resources gained from the program. For noneconomic gains a subjective weighting is necessary.

If either term in the ratio is negative there are problems of interpretation. A negative numerator and a positive denominator indicate that not only are the original costs never recovered, but in addition further losses are incurred after the conclusion of the program. On the other hand, if the numerator is positive and the denominator is negative, the program not only generates successful outcomes on its completion but also provides more resources during the program than it uses up. If both the numerator and denominator are negative this means that net gains are generated during the period of the program while net costs occur after the completion of the program. Such a situation is highly unusual.

When the numerator or the denominator of a benefit-cost ratio is negative, another combination of success and costs measure is usually more appropriate. One such combination is the net value of the gain from the program which may be expressed as:

Total Success — Total Costs

or

Average Success — Average Cost

It shows the value of the additional resources which have been

---

[1] The expression is a benefit-cost ratio when the criteria of success are measured in dollars, such as increases in participant earnings, so that both the numerator and the denominator are expressed in dollar terms. If the numerator is expressed in a unit other than dollars, such as number of persons employed or change in score on a job satisfaction scale, the expression is a cost-effectiveness ratio.

gained after costs have been deducted. It is obvious that the net value can only be calculated when both the numerator and denominator are expressed in the same units, as occurs in benefit-cost ratios. One cannot subtract apples from oranges or dollars from units gained on a satisfaction scale.

Finally, a third measure when both the numerator and denominator are expressed in dollars is the rate of return. This is the annual discount rate which will equate the total success and costs.[2] For a program to be successful, it must have a return greater than zero. To be better than an alternative program it must have a higher rate than does the alternative.

Should a Program Be Continued? The answer to this question usually depends on what alternative programs are available. General agreement, however, should exist on the discontinuation of certain types of programs. A program should be discontinued when no redeeming features are found after consideration of all criteria of success, that is, where all important dependent variables are measured and: (1) no benefit-cost ratio is greater than one, and (2) no cost-effectiveness ratio has a positive numerator or a negative denominator.

These criteria will very seldom be met if only because it will usually be impossible to quantify all of the dependent variables. Therefore, the program decisions must be based on comparisons of alternative programs.

Comparison of Alternative Programs. In a very few cases one program will be superior to another program when compared on all of the criteria we have suggested. In these cases the course of action is clear: the superior program should be expanded. (This is based on the assumption, discussed earlier, that average benefits and costs are positively related to those at the margin.) In most cases, however, one program will be superior in some areas but inferior in others. The choice of program expansion and contraction under these circumstances depends on the preferences attached to each of the goals. For example, a skill training program may be more effective than a remedial education program in raising the

---

[2] To estimate the rate of return the following equation is solved for r:

$$\sum_{t=1}^{n} \left(\frac{\text{Annual Success}}{(1 + r)t} - \frac{\text{Annual Cost}}{(1 + r)t} \right) = 0$$

Where: n = the number of years during which benefits will occur, t = the particular year considered, and r = the rate of return.

earnings and reducing the unemployment of the participants. The remedial education course, however, may lead to greater personal satisfaction and improvement in race relations. In this situation, assuming that only one program can be expanded, a choice must be made as to which is more important, increased earnings and employment or psychic and behavioral improvements. Once explicit weights showing relative importance are assigned to each of these goals, the program decisions can be made. The weights should be explicit so that others who have different values can also use the analysis.

As we discussed earlier, there are two strategies which may be followed in assigning relative weights to program goals. The first is for the decisionmaker to provide the evaluator with the weights of various goals before the evaluation is begun. The evaluator will then examine only those measures of success with non-zero weights and will aggregate his findings to arrive at a single overall measure of program effectiveness. The advantage of this approach is that it does not consider what are thought to be irrelevant goals, that is, those given no weight by the decisionmaker, and so is more economical and efficient. Its major shortcoming is that the weights assigned to goals differ among decisionmakers and over time. For this reason the alternative approach usually is more practical.

The second strategy proposes that the evaluator should calculate the benefit-cost or cost-effectiveness ratio for every goal which might be relevant for each program being examined. If consideration of all possible goals is not possible because of cost or other limitations, then the calculations should be made at least for all goals which are thought might be highly relevant. The ratios for alternative programs can then be compared in a single table.[3] This procedure allows each decision maker to assign the weights he believes are most appropriate and to arrive at a decision of overall program value. If circumstances change, the decisionmaker can redefine the weights he wishes to use and simply recalculate the relative performance of the programs. The weights should be determined independently of the analysis results, however. Otherwise there is a great post-analysis temptation to find the weights which will make the analytical results conform to previous prejudices.

Comparisons of Program Components and of the Different Groups of Participants. The same procedures could be used to compare the successes and costs of the components of a particular program. The multivariate analysis proposed includes the effects of the presence, the duration, and the quality of program components on each of the measures of success and cost.

Possibly, there may be a component which has no benefit-cost ratio greater than one and no positive cost-effectiveness ratio for all possible criteria. Such a component probably should be dropped. In some cases, however, components have to be treated as sets. For example, diagnostic testing by itself will make no improvement in the individual's behavior. Without it, however, useful counseling may be extremely difficult. More likely, however, components will vary in their effectiveness depending on the criterion of success. Once more, a tabular listing for each component can be made of the benefit-cost or cost-effectiveness ratio for each of the criterion to facilitate the choice between components.

Finally, the same method of analysis and presentation could not be used to identify the effects of different programs and components on different types of participants. The multivariate analysis would show whether programs or components produce differential success or costs depending on the types of participants. From these data benefit-cost and cost-effectiveness ratios for a particular group of participants could be calculated for all programs and components. Once more, the weighting of tabularly presented values will allow cross-program and cross-component comparisons.

---

3 Such a table might take the following form:

Criteria of Success	Benefit-Cost or Cost-Effectiveness Ratio		
	Program A	*Program B*	*Program C*
Increased production	3.0	2.0	1.0
Reduced unemployment	1 week/$1000	2 weeks/$1000	3 weeks/$1000
Increased taxes	2.0	2.0	2.0

8

CONCLUSION

A Possible Procedure for Measuring the Impact of Manpower Programs

The preceding discussion provides what may appear as a confusing number of alternative approaches to measure the benefits and costs of manpower programs. Here, we wish to compress that discussion and to outline what we feel would be a useful procedure for measuring program impact.[1]

1. The impact of all manpower programs should be systematically examined.

2. Such examinations should begin as soon as each program becomes operational and subsequently should be conducted on a regular periodic basis.

3. A sample of projects in each program should be examined. Approximately 5 percent of all projects should yield a sufficient

---

[1] Once again it should be emphasized that the procedures discussed in this primer do not represent the official policy of the Manpower Administration.

number of respondents for larger programs such as the MDTA Institutional and the NYC Out-of-School programs. For smaller programs a larger percentage of projects should be examined. The availability of project types and locations and the size of the program should influence the size and composition of the sample.

4. Projects should be selected as they are approved for funding whenever possible. This will allow for planning the study and random assignment to programs.

5. The assignment to selected projects should be made on a random basis from among those who qualify. This will be possible since there are usually more persons qualified and willing to enter manpower projects than slots available. Those who are not selected should receive the services regularly afforded by the employment service and also serve as a control group against which to measure program outcomes. The size of the control group should approximate the number of project positions for most projects. For very large projects, a sample of 200 persons should be sufficient.

Random assignment is the preferred method because it is extremely fair. After the operating agency has determined the persons who are eligible for the program, participants are selected entirely on the basis of chance. Also, this method affords a statistically valid method of determining what would have happened to the trainees if they had not entered training. It excludes the possibility of a biased control group (the persons not selected are just as highly motivated and able as those who actually enter). Without this selection procedure, a scientifically valid evaluation of a program is not possible.

6. Within one week of the start of the project an MA-101 form or other enrollment form should be completed for each person in the project and in the control group. Other information which also should be collected includes: whether a member of a farm family; address and number of Selective Service Board if a male; and addresses and telephone numbers of three persons who might know the location of the individual if he were to move. Individuals should also be given postage-free cards on which they report all changes of address.

7. During the project, records should be maintained on the nature, length, and cost of all services performed for each participant.

8. Records should also be kept for each participant on changes in his attitudes and skills during the course and his attitudes toward

the course. These should subsequently be used to develop short-term indicators of success.

9. For each person who drops out of the project, an exit interview should be conducted to determine the reasons for leaving the project and the quality and nature of his job if he leaves for this reason.

10. During the week which includes the thirtieth day after the conclusion of the project, detailed placement data should be collected on each participant in the project. These data should be evaluated as short-term measures of program success.

11. One year after the project ends, all participants in the project (or if there are more than 200, a random sample of 200 participants may be used) should be interviewed personally. Economic data for the year since the end of the project and attitudinal data should be found. The same information should be collected for the control group.

12. Multivariate analysis should be used to compare the experience and attitudes of the two groups. The comparison should show the degree of success on each criterion for the total program, for groups of participants in the program, and for various program components.

13. The economic benefits of the programs should then be projected into the future under a series of alternative assumptions.

14. At five-year intervals after the end of the project, success should be calculated again for the two groups. If sufficient funds are available, the two groups should be contacted personally. If there are limitations on funds, the Social Security Administration or Internal Revenue Service earnings histories of the two groups should be compared.

15. Calculations of costs should be made for: personnel involved in a program, local staff, and regional and national administrators; all facilities used by the program; additional expenditures required of the program participants; earnings and production lost due to program participation; payments for subsistence or reimbursements made to induce program participation; and lost tax revenues. Each of these items should be included in the calculation of the costs for society, government, the individual, or employers.

16. The costs should be calculated to include only the *additional* expenditures, resources used, or benefits foregone, i.e the difference in costs between those which occur with the program and those

which would have been incurred were there no program. This can be measured through the use of randomly selected control groups.

17. Multivariate analysis should be used to determine the effect on costs of varying participant characteristics and program components; in most cases the dependent variable would be total project costs. Attempts should be made, however, to determine the effects of program and participant changes on the costs which can be assigned to individual participants.

18. Definite attempts should be made to assign costs to the programs for which they were incurred and to include all costs even though there were no funds transferred.

19. Success and cost calculations should be combined for each criterion of program success. We suggest that benefit-cost and cost-effectiveness ratios are convenient comparison measures.

20. Programs which have no benefit-cost ratio greater than one or positive cost-effectiveness ratio should be reappraised. The relative merits of other programs should be judged by means of tabular presentation of the ratios for all criteria and by assignment of weights to each criterion. This procedure should be applied in the same manner to make judgments about program components and optimal assignment of individuals to programs.

Limitations on Evaluation Techniques

There are three basic limitations on the impact evaluation methods we have presented which should always be kept in mind.

First, the analysis will be based on only some of the criteria of success and only some of the costs of manpower programs. Our lists of criteria and costs are admittedly incomplete. Even if more were added to each list, however, constraints on time, funds, and ability would limit the material which could be considered. Important criteria might be omitted. More important, however, we consider only those criteria of success and costs which can be measured. We ignore those which cannot be measured, such as the effects of manpower programs on persons not in the program.[2] For these reasons the judgments which are made about programs, components, and participants may not always be "right."

Second, even for measureable criteria, correct evaluations of

---

[2] We have attempted, however, to indicate the areas where quantification is necessary and possible, such as in the measurement of satisfaction and the measurement of second-party effects.

manpower programs cannot always be designed. We have argued that random selection of experimental and control groups will permit considerably more accurate and trustworthy evaluations than will other methods of sample selection. There are still problems involved, however. The possible interaction of control and experimental groups is one; another is that only the best estimate of effects of a program are presented. While ranges can be established into which the true value is likely to fall, a 100 percent confidence level cannot be achieved.

There also is no way to determine true cause and effect. Not all variables which could conceivably influence the outcomes and costs of manpower programs can be included in any analysis. Therefore, an observed relationship may be due to some other factor which is correlated with the two variables being examined. For example, it may be found that on-the-job training has higher ratios than does institutional training. If, however, the institutional courses are predominantly in depressed areas while the OJT courses are in labor shortage areas, and the local unemployment rate is not a variable in the analysis, the return to OJT training might fall if that program replaced all institutional courses. Likewise, we measure relationships which exist for a given period of time. They may change over time as other unanalyzed variables change. Thus while the ratios obtained from the types of analyses presented are precise, their precision should be examined with a jaundiced eye. An estimate can be no better than the assumptions on which it is built.

The third limitation has been discussed before. The estimates of success and costs proposed here are averages for the programs. They do not measure directly the effect of changes in program size. Thus while one program may have considerably higher ratios than does another, increasing the size of that program may lead to smaller gains in success per dollar of cost than increasing the program which has lower average ratios. Until further information is available, we can only assume that the effects of changing the size of programs will be directly related to their ratios of success to costs.

A Final Word for Impact Evaluation

The type of analysis we have proposed is difficult to conduct, obviously filled with pitfalls, and may not be correct when completed. There are reasons for its use, however. It forces those responsible for manpower program decisions to attach weights to their goals and to quantify the success and costs of a program as far as is possible, rather than rest content with vague qualitative judgments and personal hunches. This is obviously a good thing in itself; some information is better than none. Also, it has a very valuable byproduct of causing questions to be asked which would otherwise not have been raised. Thus even though this type of evaluation may not always give the "right" answers, if used sensibly it may lead to the asking of more "right" questions. And as experience and expertise are accumulated, this method should also lead to better answers.[3]

---

[3] A. R. Prest and R. Turvey, "Cost-Benefit Analysis: A Survey," *Surveys of Economic Theory*, New York: St. Marins Press, 1966, p. 202.

SELECTED BIBLIOGRAPHY

Bateman, Worth. "An Application of Cost-Benefit Analysis to the Work Experience Program," *American Economic Review.* Papers and Proceedings of the Seventy-Ninth Meeting of the American Economic Association, Vol. 57, No. 2, May 1967, pp. 80-90.

Bateman, Worth. "Assessing Program Effectiveness," *Welfare in Review.* January-February 1968, pp. 1-10.

Borus, Michael E. "A Benefit-Cost Analysis of the Economic Effectiveness of Retraining the Unemployed," *Yale Economic Essays.* Vol. 4, No. 2, 1964, pp. 371-429.

Borus, Michael E. "Time Trends in the Benefits from Retraining in Connecticut," *Proceedings of the Twentieth Annual Winter Meeting.* Industrial Relations Research Association, Madison, Wisconsin, 1968, pp. 36-46.

Cain, Glen G. *Benefit/Cost Estimates for Job Corps.* Institute for Research on Poverty, University of Wisconsin, Madison, 1968.

Cain, Glen G., and Robinson G. Hollister. "The Methodology of Evaluating Social Action Programs," *Public-Private Manpower*

Policies. Industrial Relations Research Association, Madison, Wisconsin, 1969, pp. 5-34.

Caroll, Adger B., and Loren A. Ihnen. *Costs and Returns of Technical Education: A Pilot Study.* Prepared for Manpower Administration, U. S. Department of Labor, Washington, D. C., 1966.

Chase, Samuel B., Jr., ed. *Problems in Public Expenditure Analysis.* The Brookings Institution, Washington, D. C., 1968.

Dorfman, Robert, ed. *Measuring Benefits of Government Investments.* The Brookings Institution, Washington, D. C., 1965.

Eckerman, William C., Eva K. Gerstel, and Richard B. Williams. *A Comprehensive Assessment of the Problems and Characteristics of the Neighborhood Youth Corps Enrollees: A Pilot Investigation.* Prepared for the Manpower Administration, U. S. Department of Labor, Washington, D. C., 1968.

Gurin, Gerald. *A National Attitude Study of Trainees in MDTA Institutional Programs.* Prepared for the Manpower Administration, U. S. Department of Labor, Washington, D. C., 1968.

Hall, George E. "Recent Census Bureau Experience with Longitudinal Surveys," *Proceedings of Social Statistics Section, 1968.* American Statistical Association, Washington, D. C., 1968.

Hardin, Einar, and Michael E. Borus. "An Economic Evaluation of the Retraining Program in Michigan: Methodological Problems of Research," *Proceedings of Social Statistics Section, 1966.* American Statistical Association, Washington, D. C., 1966, pp. 133-37.

Hardin, Einar, and Michael E. Borus. *Economic Benefits and Costs of Retraining Courses in Michigan.* Prepared for the Manpower Administration, U. S. Department of Labor, Washington, D. C., 1969.

John, Julius A. *The Measurement of Costs, Utilization and Effectiveness of Social Welfare Programs.* University of Pennsylvania School of Social Work, Research Center, Philadelphia, 1965.

Joint Economic Committee. *The Analysis and Evaluation of Public Expenditures: The PPB System.* A Compendium of Papers Submitted to the Subcommittee on Economy in Government, Washington, D. C., 1969.

Joint Economic Committee. *Economic Analysis of Public Investment Decisions: Interest Rate Policy and Discounting Analysis.* Report of the Subcommittee on Economy in Government, Washington, D. C., 1968.

Levine, Abraham S. "Cost-Benefit Analysis and Social Welfare—An Exploration of Possible Applications," *Welfare in Review*. Vol. 4, No. 2, February 1966, pp. 1-11.

Levine, Abraham S. "Evaluation Program Effectiveness and Efficiency—Rationale and Description of Research in Progress," *Welfare in Review*. Vol. 5, No. 2, February 1967, pp. 1-11.

Levinson, Perry. "Evaluation of Social Welfare Programs—Two Research Models," *Welfare in Review*. Vol. 4, No. 12, December 1966, pp. 5-11.

Louis Harris and Associates. *A Continuing Study of Job Corps Terminations Wave II—Initial Interview with Terminations from October 15, 1966, to December 15, 1966*. Prepared for the Office of Economic Opportunity, Washington, D. C., 1967.

MacDonald, John S. "Benefit-Cost Analysis of Social Welfare Programs," *Proceedings of the Seventeenth Annual Meeting*. Industrial Relations Research Association, Madison, Wisconsin, 1965, pp. 186-94.

Mahoney, W. M. *Cost Benefit Evaluation of Welfare Demonstration Projects*. Research Management Corporation Report UR-040, Bethesda, Maryland, 1968.

Main, Earl D. "A Nationwide Evaluation of M.D.T.A. Institutional Job Training," *The Journal of Human Resources*, Vol. III, No. 2, 1968, pp. 159-70.

Mangum, Garth L. *MDTA: Foundation of Federal Manpower Policy*. The John Hopkins Press, Baltimore, 1968.

McCall, J. J. *An Analysis of Poverty: A Suggested Methodology*. Prepared for Office of Economic Opportunity, Washington, D. C., 1968.

Muir, Allen H., Leslie Appleton, Marcus Kaplan, and Curtis Knight. *Cost Effectiveness Analysis of On-the-Job and Institutional Training Courses*. Prepared for the Manpower Administration, U.S. Department of Labor, Washington, D.C., 1967.

Operations Research Incorporated. *Manpower Evaluation Study*. Prepared for the Office of Economic Opportunity, Washington, D. C., 1968.

Orcutt, Guy H., and Alice G. Orcutt. "Incentive and Disincentive Experimentation for Income Maintenance Policy Purposes," *American Economic Review*. Vol. 58, No. 4, September 1968, pp. 754-72.

Prest, A. R., and Ralph Turvey. "Cost-Benefit Analysis: A Survey,"

Surveys of Economic Theory, Vol. III, St. Martin's Press, New York, 1967.

Resource Management Corporation. *Cost-Benefit Evaluation of Welfare Demonstration Projects: A Test Application to Juvenile Rehabilitation.* Prepared for the Department of Health, Education, and Welfare, Washington, D. C., 1968.

Resource Management Corporation. *The Feasibility of Benefit-Cost Analysis in the War on Poverty: A Test Application to Manpower Programs.* Prepared for the General Accounting Office, Washington, D. C., 1968.

Ribich, Thomas I. *Education and Poverty.* The Brookings Institution, Washington, D. C., 1968.

Robin, Gerald D. *An Assessment of the In-Public School Neighborhood Youth Corps Projects in Cincinnati and Detroit, with Special Reference to Summer-Only and Year-Round Enrollees.* Prepared for the Manpower Administration, U. S. Department of Labor, Washington, D. C., 1969.

Sewell, David O. "Critique of Cost-Benefit Analyses of Training," *Monthly Labor Review.* Vol. 90, No. 9, September 1967, pp. 45-54.

Shab, B. V. *A Developmental Study for an Index of Underemployment.* Research Triangle Institute, Research Triangle Park, N. C., 1968.

Sherwood, Clarence C. "Methodological Measurement and Social Action Considerations Related to Assessments of Large Scale Demonstration Programs," *Proceedings of Social Statistics Section.* American Statistical Association, Washington, D. C., 1965, pp. 199-207.

Somers, Gerald G., ed. *Retraining the Unemployed.* University of Wisconsin Press, Madison, 1968.

Somers, Gerald G., and Graeme H. McKechnie. "Vocational Retraining Programs for the Unemployed," *Proceedings of the Twentieth Annual Winter Meeting.* Industrial Relations Research Association, Madison, Wisconsin, 1968, pp. 25-35.

Somers, Gerald G., and Ernst W. Stomsdorfer. "A Benefit-Cost Analysis of Manpower Retraining," *Proceedings of the Seventeenth Annual Meeting.* Industrial Relations Research Association, Madison, Wisconsin, 1965, pp. 172-85.

Somers, Gerald G., and W. Donald Wood, eds. *Cost-Benefit Analysis of Manpower Policies.* Industrial Relations Center, Queens University and Center for Studies in Technical and Vocational

Education, University of Wisconsin, Madison, 1969.

Spiegelman, R. G. "A Benefit/Cost Model to Evaluate Education Programs," *Socio-Economic Planning Science,* Vol. 1, 1968.

Stromsdorfer, Ernst. "Determinants of Economic Success in Retraining the Unemployed: The West Virginia Experience," *The Journal of Human Resources,* Vol. III, No. 2, 1968, pp. 139-58.

Suchman, Edward A. *Evaluative Research: Principles and Practice in Public Service and Social Action Programs.* Russell Sage Foundation, New York, 1967.

Walther, Regis H., Margaret Magnusson, and Shirley Cherkasky. *A Study of the Effectiveness of Selected Out-of-School Neighborhood Youth Corps Programs.* George Washington University Social Research Group, Washington, D. C., 1968.

Weisbrod, Burton A. "Conceptual Issues in Evaluating Training Programs," *Monthly Labor Review,* Vol. 89, No. 10, October 1966, pp. 1091-97.